Essential
Ireland

by

BRIGID AVISON

Brigid Avison is a writer and editor with several
years' experience of guide book
publishing.

AA

Produced by AA Publishing

Written by Brigid Avison
Peace and Quiet section
by Paul Sterry
Series Adviser: Ingrid Morgan
Series Controller: Nia Williams
Copy Editor: Antonia Hebbert

Edited, designed and produced by
AA Publishing. Maps © The
Automobile Association 1992.

Distributed in the United Kingdom
by the Publishing Division of The
Automobile Association, Fanum
House, Basingstoke, Hampshire,
RG21 2EA.

The contents of this publication are
believed correct at the time of
printing. Nevertheless, the
publishers cannot accept
responsibility for errors or
omissions, nor for changes in details
given. We have tried to ensure
accuracy in this guide, but things
do change and we would be
grateful if readers would advise us
of any inaccuracies they may
encounter.

A CIP catalogue record for this
book is available from the British
Library.

ISBN 0 7495 0308 4

Published by The Automobile
Association.

Typesetting: Avonset, Midsomer
Norton, Bath
Colour separation: LC Repro,
Aldermaston

Printed in Italy by Printers SRL,
Trento

Front cover picture: Connemara

80,000-strong force called the Irish Volunteers won concessions for the Irish parliament. More radical, republican demands were expressed by the Society of United Irishmen, led by Theobald Wolfe Tone. For a while the British government tried to reduce popular discontent by restoring land ownership and other civil rights to Catholics. Violent clashes followed, and the United Irishmen attempted two rebellions. The century ended with the abolition of the Irish parliament, by the Act of Union in 1800. The last flicker of the flames of revolt, Robert Emmet's attempt to seize Dublin Castle in 1803, was easily smothered.

Emancipation and Emigration

The Act of Union won support from Irish Catholic leaders on the assurance that it would be swiftly followed by a change of law, allowing Catholics to sit in parliament in London. When this did not materialise, 'emancipation' became the rallying cry of Daniel O'Connell, a Catholic lawyer from Co Kerry, who created the first popular mass movement in Ireland's political history. This goal achieved, the Liberator – as he became known – began a campaign based on non-violent mass protest for the repeal of the Union. But political events were overtaken by disaster when, for three successive years, the staple food of Irish peasants, the potato, was hit by blight. Unable to afford other food, they starved – even though Irish grain and meat were being exported to England. Countless families were evicted because they could not pay their rents, and whole communities disappeared. Out of a total population of around eight million, some one million died and another million or more emigrated. The next individual to take centre stage was Charles Stuart Parnell, a Protestant landowner who championed the cause of Irish independence, or 'Home Rule'. The general election of 1885 gave Parnell's party the balance of power in parliament, and Home Rule seemed almost won. But Parnell's career – and the Home Rule campaign – ended in ruins after he was named as co-respondent in a divorce case, brought for political reasons by Captain William O'Shea, whose wife Kitty had borne three of Parnell's children. Parnell died in 1891, a tragic figure, whose fate, according to the poet W B Yeats, finally convinced many Irish people of the uselessness of parliamentary politics as a route to independence.

Rising tension in the early 1900s came to a head in the 1916 Easter Rising, when Padraic Pearse led an attack on the General Post Office and read out a proclamation of a new Irish republic. The rising involved only about 2,000 people and failed to attract popular support, but repressive action by the British government ensured that it was not forgotten. The following years are a story of guerilla warfare, oppression, negotiation and civil war. Finally, in 1923, a treaty was agreed which established the Irish Free State, but excluded six of Ulster's nine counties.

This treaty drew the border which exists today between Northern Ireland and the Republic – as the Free State became in 1948. The new state wrestled with problems of a different sort in the economic slump of the 1920s and 1930s, but a sense of national identity was fostered by policies such as making Irish the first official language. In 1958 Sean Lemass became Taioseach (prime minister), and began to encourage foreign investment, to create jobs for young people. The Republic joined the European Community in 1972, and greeted the 1990s by electing Mrs Mary Robinson as its first female president.

Over the border, Northern Ireland has had a bad press in recent years because of sectarian violence, originating deep in Irish history but sparked off by tension between Protestants and the Catholic minority in 1968–9. Sectarian terrorist groups burgeoned, and still exist – it is worth stressing, though, that Northern Ireland is a safe as well as beautiful place for visitors.

A Literary Renaissance

A counterpart to these events has been a flowering of literary talent. One of the senators of the Irish Free State was W B

Yeats, whose poetry ranks among the best and still draws literary pilgrims to the places in Co Sligo that inspired him. Together with Lady Augusta Gregory and others, Yeats also helped set up the Abbey Theatre in Dublin, where early productions included works by Sean O'Casey and J M Synge. Another of Yeats's contemporaries was Oscar Wilde, who was born in Dublin and educated at Enniskillen and Trinity College.

The dominant figure of 20th-century Irish literature is James Joyce, whose vast and complex novel *Ulysses* was published in 1922. It recreates a single day – 16 June 1904 – in Dublin. Other 20th-century Irish writers make an impressive list – including Samuel Beckett among the playwrights, the poets Louis MacNeice, Patrick Kavanagh and Seamus Heaney, and among the novelists, Flann O'Brien, William Trevor and Brian Moore. Ireland's wealth of literature gives visitors an enticing way to taste Irish culture and get a feel for this complex and compelling island as it approaches the 21st century.

... And Parnell loved his country, And Parnell loved his lass.

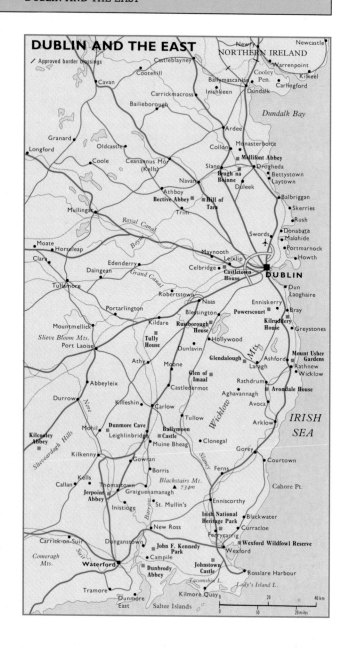

DUBLIN AND THE EAST

DUBLIN

Like many capital cities, Dublin manages to be the pivot of its country's life while also standing apart from it. Dubliners have a tendency to see themselves as a special breed – a tendency which is not unnoticed, or unresented, by their fellow Irish. Their city is certainly the largest and most cosmopolitan in Ireland, its urbanity a striking contrast to an otherwise largely rural society. But Dubliners, unlike the inhabitants of many large, anonymous cities, are usually more than ready to chat to strangers, giving the visitor ample opportunity to relish one of their immediate distinctions, the captivating Dublin accent. The essential Dublin for visitors lies within a compact, easily walked area. Most of the galleries, museums and important public buildings lie in the area south of the River Liffey. Georgian houses grand and small, many with exquisite doorcases, are to be found all over the city, often in an astonishingly dilapidated state. The best-preserved areas are to the south of Trinity College, notably Merrion Square (note the wall plaques commemorating famous occupants) and Fitzwilliam Square.

This century has seen the destruction of much of Georgian Dublin; sadly, little of Dublin's modern architecture justifies the loss. Decay remains evident even in the heart of the city, in run-down districts where street crimes such as mugging are a real danger; the most notorious are round Christ Church and St Patrick's cathedrals, and the northwest area round Connolly Station, Gardiner and Summerhill Streets.

Even so, Dublin is a city of great charm and often beauty, with every sort of attraction for visitors, including outstanding museums and galleries, plenty of excellent shops and restaurants and first-class entertainment – a good choice as 1991 European City of Culture.

It also has a beautiful setting, in easy reach of both the Wicklow Mountains and the coast. One of the best ways in and out of the city on the coastal side is the DART, the rapid transit rail service that runs from Howth, southwards down to Bray.

Four Courts and the Liffey at night

WHAT TO SEE IN THE CITY CENTRE

♦♦
BANK OF IRELAND
College Green
This splendid 18th-century Classical building was designed to house the Irish parliament. Begun in 1729 to designs by Sir Edward Lovett Pearce, and extended in the 1780s by James Gandon, it was made redundant in 1800 by the Act of Union. Following its sale in 1803 to the Bank of Ireland, it underwent extensive internal alterations, but Pearce's House of Lords survives, with its 18th-century tapestries and resplendent Waterford glass chandelier.

♦♦
CHRIST CHURCH CATHEDRAL
Christ Church Place
The early Gothic cathedral dates back to the 1170s, when it replaced a timber church; but a lot of it was rebuilt during restoration in the 1870s. Original medieval parts include the transepts and the huge crypt, once used as taverns and now housing many fragments of stonework. More fine stonework decorates the great nave.

♦
CIVIC MUSEUM
South William Street
Maps, pictures and models tell the story of Dublin's history. The house itself was built in 1765–71 for the Society of Artists and later used by the City Assembly.

DUBLIN

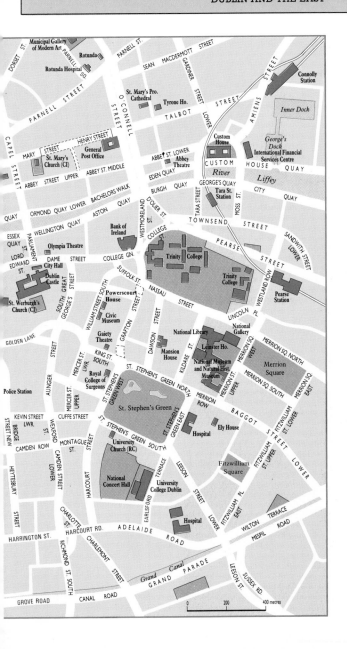

DUBLIN AND THE EAST

◆◆◆
DUBLIN CASTLE
Lord Edward Street
Built by the Normans in the early 13th century, in Elizabeth I's reign the castle became the English viceroy's residence, remaining the official headquarters of the British administration until 1922. Much of it is 18th-century, including the richly decorated **State Apartments**, some with particularly fine plasterwork. The **Church of the Holy Trinity** (1807–14), formerly the Chapel Royal, is a masterpiece of neo-Gothic design by Francis Johnston, with a gorgeously ornate yet intimate interior.

◆
DUBLIN WRITERS' MUSEUM
Parnell Square
Two restored Georgian houses are the setting for this new centre, combining a library of

State Drawing Room, Dublin Castle

rare books, exhibitions and memorabilia of many of Dublin's most famous writers.

◆◆
FOUR COURTS
Inns Quay
With its vast columns and copper-covered dome, the courts building is a lasting monument to Dublin's civic pride and prosperity in the late 18th century. It was shelled in 1922 during the civil war; the exterior emerged largely unscathed, though the ensuing fire destroyed most of the archives in the adjacent Record Office. The restored interior now contains 10 courts, including the Supreme Court. The architect was James Gandon, who completed work begun by Thomas Cooley; another of his magnificent designs, the **Custom House**, stands further downstream, and is reckoned one of Ireland's finest buildings.

◆
MARSH'S LIBRARY
next to St Patrick's Cathedral
Built in around 1702 for Archbishop Narcissus Marsh, this is Ireland's oldest public library. Its carefully restored interior houses a precious collection of books and manuscripts.

◆◆
MUNICIPAL GALLERY OF MODERN ART
Parnell Square North
A fine 18th-century townhouse provides an elegant setting for a superb collection of modern paintings, many of them

bequeathed by Sir Hugh Lane (1875–1915), as well as some impressive sculpture. Artists represented here include Manet, Monet, Corot and Augustus John, Henry Moore and several Irish painters including Lavery, O'Conor and Jack Yeats.

◆◆◆
NATIONAL GALLERY
Merrion Square West
The gallery's collection represents every major school of European painting, as well as many memorable works by Irish painters. Several rooms are devoted to Italian art; others to the Flemish, Dutch and German collections (including works by Jan Steen, Rembrandt and Lucas Cranach the Elder), the Spanish collection (including El Greco, Murillo and Goya) and a small selection of 18th- to 19th-century British art. A wing added in the 1960s houses French and modern paintings. Portraits include those of national figures such as Swift, Parnell and Joyce, and also W B and Jack Yeats, painted by their father John.

◆◆◆
NATIONAL MUSEUM AND LIBRARY
Kildare Street
The star attraction of the **Museum** is the Treasury, which has two 8th-century masterpieces of Celtic metalwork, the Tara Brooch and Ardagh Chalice. Also here are the Shrine of St Patrick's Bell and the Cross of Cong, both 12th-century. Among other remarkable

exhibits are several richly decorated and jewelled book shrines.
Other displays include Dublin 1000, combining artefacts and models to illustrate Irish life in Viking and Norman times; collections of ceramics, silver and glass, musical instruments and Japanese antiquities; and exhibitions on the 1916 Rising and War of Independence.
The **Library** opposite has extensive collections of Irish maps, prints and newspapers as well as many first editions.

◆◆
NATURAL HISTORY MUSEUM
Upper Merrion Street
This fascinating and somehow nightmarish collection – stuffed, mounted, pickled or pinned, as necessary – includes a comprehensive

Ireland's National Gallery

survey of native Irish species of birds, mammals, fishes and insects, together with other species from around the world, crammed into two floors and two encircling galleries.

◆
POWERSCOURT HOUSE
South William Street
The 1770s mansion, which has some fine plasterwork, now forms part of an attractive shopping development, with a central glass-roofed courtyard overlooked by cafés and restaurants. As well as shops, there is a small gallery run by the Crafts Council of Ireland, with changing exhibitions.

◆
ST MICHAN'S CHURCH
Church Street
The church was restored in the 19th century, but still has some 18th-century features, such as a finely carved organ (1724) on which Handel is supposed to have performed. Tours include a visit to the limestone vaults, where mummified corpses lie.

◆◆
ST PATRICK'S CATHEDRAL
Patrick Street
Monuments in abundance are the highlight of this cathedral. Dating from the early 13th century, it was restored in the 1860s, though much of the choir is original. St Patrick's houses the bones of 18th-century satirist Jonathan Swift, who served as its dean from 1713 until his death in 1745. For a reminder of his acerbic style, read the epitaph he wrote for the Duke of Schomberg, in the north choir aisle.

◆◆◆
TRINITY COLLEGE AND LIBRARY
College Green
The handsome main front of the college dates from 1759, but Dublin's university was founded by Elizabeth I in 1591. It remained a bastion of the Protestant establishment until 1873 when religious restrictions were lifted; 30 years later, female students were admitted. Former students include many of the great names of Irish history and culture, from Congreve to Wilde to Beckett, Burke to Wolfe Tone. From June to September, there are guided tours of the campus (ask at the front entrance).

Trinity's main gateway leads into Parliament Square, a cobbled quadrangle flanked by the **Examination Hall**, or Theatre, and the **Chapel**, both dating from the late 18th century, with notably fine stucco decoration. The **Dining Hall**, 1743, contains a number of portraits. The **Library**, on the right of the second quadrangle, was built in 1712–32. The main library, called the Long Room, stretches 209 feet (64m), divided down each side into 19 bays on two levels, flanked by marble busts. The library's collection was begun in 1601, and includes many rare manuscripts, the most famous being the Book of Kells. This anonymous masterpiece, created in around AD800 in the monastery of Kells in Co Meath, has been re-bound in four volumes, and part is on display (but be prepared for crowds). Other manuscripts on display may include the Book of Durrow (7th-century, the oldest in the collection) and the Book of Dimma; also there is a medieval Irish harp. As a contrast to all this history, Paul Koralek's **Arts Building** (1980) and **New Library** (1968) are modern structures of concrete, Wicklow granite and plate glass, but fit in well. The oldest remaining part of the college is the **Rubrics** (1690). The third quadrangle is New Square, where the highlights are the delightful **Doric Printing House** (1734) and the **Museum Building**, with an imposing entrance hall and staircase. On leaving the university, look left of the main entrance for the **Provost's House** (1760).

WHAT TO SEE BEYOND THE CITY CENTRE

◆◆
CHESTER BEATTY LIBRARY
20 Shrewsbury Road, Ballsbridge
Donated to his adopted homeland by an American mining millionaire, this internationally important book and manuscript collection ranges from Biblical papyri and exquisite Books of Hours to Persian and Turkish Korans and Indian miniatures. Only a fraction is on display at any one time. Items from the extensive collection of Chinese and Japanese objects may also be seen, including snuff-bottles, carved seals and netsukes.

Trinity College

◆
DALKEY
nine miles (14km) southeast
A popular resort that retains its charm. In the main street are the remains of two 15th- to 16th-century fortified mansions and a ruined ancient church, St Begnet's. In summer, boats run to Dalkey Island, a bird sanctuary with a Martello tower and another ancient church. There are fine views of Killiney Bay, Bray Head and the Sugar Loaf Hills from the park on Sorrento Point.

◆◆
GUINNESS BREWERY
Crane Street
A visit is a chance to learn from displays and an audio-visual show about the history and manufacture of Dublin's most famous product – the near-black Guinness beer. At the end you can remind yourself of its taste in a pleasant bar. The samples are covered by the entrance fee and amount to the cheapest Guinness you will find in its native city (children get soft drinks instead).

◆◆
HOWTH PENINSULA
nine miles (14km) northeast
Originally an island, the peninsula of Howth (rhymes with 'growth') is now a well-heeled residential district with two golf courses. In summer it draws flocks of Dubliners and tourists to enjoy the beaches and views. The attractive hillside town of **Howth** overlooks a large, busy artificial harbour and in summer, boats run to **Ireland's Eye**, a bird sanctuary. Howth's older buildings include the Abbey and the College. A spectacular cliff path leads from the town round the headland to Baily lighthouse. A short walk west of the town is the much altered and extended 15th-century **Howth Castle**. Its gardens include an early 18th-century formal garden, and are at their best in early summer.

◆
JAMES JOYCE'S TOWER
Sandycove, Dun Laoghaire
James Joyce stayed in the Martello tower briefly, and not very enjoyably, when it was home to his fellow writer, Oliver St John Gogarty, and used it as the setting for the first chapter of *Ulysses*. It now houses a small museum of first editions, letters and Joycean memorabilia. Beside it are a small sandy beach and the Forty Foot, a rocky diving area traditionally reserved for men.

◆◆
KILMAINHAM GAOL
Inchicore Road, Kilmainham
A powerfully atmospheric place, this grim building dates back to 1796. Its last prisoner, before it closed in 1924, was Eamon de Valera, later Taoiseach and President of Ireland. It was he who opened it in 1966 as a museum commemorating the many political prisoners who spent time in its cells and exercise yards – and, in the case of the leaders of the 1916 Rising, met their deaths there.
Near by, on the south bank of the Liffey, is another memorial,

the **Memorial Park**, dedicated to the 49,000 Irish who died in the 1914–18 war.

Kilmainham Gaol is now a museum

♦♦
MARINO CASINO
Malahide Road, Marino
The 'casino' is a perfect little Palladian pavilion, dating from the 1760s. It was designed by Sir William Chambers as a pleasurehouse for the Earl of Charlemont.

♦
NATIONAL BOTANIC GARDENS
Glasnevin, off N2
Founded in 1795, the Gardens include a superb collection of Victorian glasshouses (which may be closed, as they are being restored), most of them the work of Dublin ironmaster Richard Turner. The 20,000

and more varieties of plants include rare shrubs and trees; the many features include rose, bog and pond gardens. In nearby **Prospect Cemetery** are the graves of Parnell, O'Connell and Gerard Manley Hopkins, who is buried in the plot reserved for Jesuits.

♦
NATIONAL MARITIME MUSEUM
Dun Laoghaire
Housed in an 1837 Mariners' Church, the museum includes a large collection of models, the optical system from Baily lighthouse on the Howth peninsula, and a 35-foot (11m) French longboat captured in Bantry Bay, Co Cork, in 1796.

♦♦♦
PHOENIX PARK
Parkgate Street
Embracing over 1,752 acres (709 hectares), the park was mainly laid out in the 18th century, during the viceroyalty of Lord Chesterfield. He erected the Phoenix Column not far from the spring that gave the park its name (a corruption of the Gaelic *fionn uisce*, meaning 'clear water'). Attractions include the **People's Garden** with a small lake; and the **Zoological Gardens**, one of the oldest zoos in the world. The Park also contains the official residence of the President of Ireland; the US Ambassador's residence; and a racecourse, polo fields and several playing fields.

♦♦
ROYAL HOSPITAL
Kilmainham Lane, Kilmainham
The home of the new Irish Museum of Modern Art, this magnificent building was designed by William Robinson in the 1680s to house retired and disabled soldiers, following the style of Les Invalides in Paris. Thoroughly restored during the 1980s, it now looks much as it did in the early 19th century. The rooms around the large arcaded courtyard include a great dining hall (sometimes closed for private functions) and a baroque chapel, decorated with an extraordinary plasterwork ceiling – not the original but a faithful copy – and fine wood carving.

Accommodation
At all levels, from luxury hotels to hostels, accommodation in Dublin is roughly twice the price of equivalents elsewhere in the Republic. It is always sensible to make advance reservations, and essential if your visit coincides with one of the main sporting events or festivals.
Telephone numbers in Dublin are changing. Check with Directory Enquiries, tel: 190.

Phoenix Park – the city's lungs

Expensive:
Blooms 3-star, Anglesea Street, Dublin 2 (tel: (01) 715622) – medium-sized, modern hotel in Temple Bar district.
Shelbourne 4-star, St Stephen's Green, Dublin 2 (tel: (01) 766471) – central, traditional-style 'grand hotel', now part of the Trusthouse Forte group.

Medium:
Ashling 3-star, Parkgate Street, Dublin 8 (tel: (01) 772324) – medium-sized, family run, close to Phoenix Park.
Lansdowne, Pembroke Road, Ballsbridge, Dublin 4 (tel: (01) 682522) – small, on busy road in residential/business district.
Mont Clare, Merrion Square, Dublin 2 (tel: (01) 616799) – new addition to the city centre's smart hotels.

Cheap:
All are guesthouses unless otherwise indicated.

In the city centre:
The Fitzwilliam, 41 Fitzwilliam Street Upper, Dublin 2 (tel: (01) 600448) and **Georgian House**, 20 Lower Baggot Street, Dublin 2 (tel: (01) 618832) – both in the heart of Georgian Dublin, with en-suite bathrooms; and further south, **Kilronan House**, 70 Adelaide Road, Dublin 2 (tel: (01) 755266).

In the suburbs:
Abrae Court, 9 Zion Road, Rathgar, Dublin 6 (tel: (01) 979944) and **Ariel House**, 52 Lansdowne Road, Ballsbridge, Dublin 4 (tel: (01) 685512) – in converted Victorian villas, the latter close to the sport stadium and a DART station. **Avondale**

House (T&C), Scribblestown, Castleknock, Co Dublin (tel: (01) 386545) – an elegant house close to Phoenix Park. **The Beddington**, 181–2 Rathgar Road, Dublin 6 (tel: (01) 978047) – a large house set back from the main road. **Egans House**, 7/9 Iona Park, Glasnevin, Dublin 9 (tel: (01) 303611) and its neighbour, **Iona House**, 5 Iona Park (tel: (01) 306217) – both comfortable family-run guesthouses in a quiet suburb. **Mount Herbert**, 1 Herbert Road, Lansdowne Road, Ballsbridge, Dublin 4 (tel: (01) 684321) – a competitively priced hotel in a quiet road close to the sport stadium and a DART station. **Raglan Lodge**, 10 Raglan Road, Ballsbridge, Dublin 4 (tel: (01) 606697) – all bedrooms with private bathrooms. **St Aiden's Guest House**, 32 Brighton Road, Rathgar, Dublin 6 (tel: (01) 902011) – another well-modernised Victorian house.

Restaurants
A good area for a range of prices and types is the lively Temple Bar district. Several of the establishments listed below are out of the centre, but quickly reached by car, cab or, in some cases, DART. The *Irish Times* carries occasional restaurant reviews in its Saturday edition. Most of the smarter restaurants are closed on Sundays.

Expensive:
King Sitric, East Pier, Howth (tel: (01) 325235) – famous for its seafood with a delightful harbour side setting; dinner only.

Park, 40 Main Street, Blackrock (tel: (01) 866177) – elegant setting for excellent, mainly modern French meals; also good-value fixed-price lunches.

Restaurant Na Mara, Harbour Road, Dun Laoghaire (tel: (01) 806767) – seafood restaurant in splendid station building.

Medium:
Ayumi-Ya, Newpark Centre, Newtownpark Avenue, Blackrock (tel: (01) 831767) – authentic Japanese food.

Eastern Tandoori, 34–5 South William Street (tel: (01) 710428), also in Blackrock (tel: (01) 892856) – reckoned by many the best Indian food in Dublin, one central and one suburban.

La Pigalle, 14 Temple Bar (tel: (01) 719262) – good-value French cooking in simply furnished restaurant, popular at lunchtime with journalists, lawyers and business people.

Rajdoot Tandoori, Westbury Centre, Clarendon Street (tel: (01) 794274) – rivals Eastern Tandoori for best Indian food.

Cheap:
A Dublin institution for over a century, **Bewley's Cafés** now have four city-centre establishments, usually open into the early evening, in South Great George Street, Mary Street, Grafton Street and Westmoreland Street. Other good central places for lunch or a daytime snack are:

Fitzers National Gallery Restaurant, Merrion Square West; the justly popular **Kilkenny Design Centre** restaurant, Nassau Street; **Mitchell's Cellars**, 21 Kildare Street, a sophisticated lunchtime-only wine bar; and, of the many eateries in the Powerscourt Town House shopping centre, South William Street, the **Periwinkle Seafood Bar** and **Blazing Salads**. For Sunday brunch, there's the **Royal Hospital**, Kilmainham; or try Chinese *dim sum* in the **Imperial**, Wicklow Street (tel: (01) 772580).

In the Temple Bar district, lively places popular with younger people include the **Bad Ass Café**, 9–10 Crown Alley, off Dame Street, and the nearby, trendier **Elephant and Castle**, 18 Temple Bar. For something different, there's **The Boxty House**, 20 Temple Bar, whose Irish dishes include variations on boxty, a sort of potato pancake. *The* place for fish and chips is **Leo Burdock's**, in Werburgh Street near Christ Church.

Entertainment
Live entertainment, particularly music and theatre, is one of Dublin's greatest attractions. For an informal night out, there are the pubs, some of which have traditional or other live music in the evenings. Details of these and venues for all kinds of entertainment can be found in *In Dublin* magazine, or in the tourist board's *What's On In Dublin*. The Friday edition of the *Evening Press* has details of folk music; and Comhaltas Ceoltóirí Eireann, Belgrave Square, Monkstown (tel: (01) 800295) can tell you about venues for traditional Irish music and dance in Dublin and

the rest of Ireland (the pronunciation is 'coaltas keoltori ayran'). The *Irish Times* has a daily 'What's On Today' round-up by county, and lists special events on Saturdays; and the Wednesday issue carries reviews of current plays, films and concerts.

Shopping

The main upmarket shopping district is the area south of the Liffey, around Grafton Street (part of which is closed to traffic) and Dawson Street. In Nassau Street, the **Kilkenny Design Centre** has a good selection of Irish products including Donegal tweed, pottery and jewellery; and the **Powerscourt Town House** centre in South William Street includes several crafts and antiques shops. Other places to find craft goods are the **Tower Design Craft Centre** in Pearse Street and at **Marley Park** in the southern suburb of Rathfarnham. Good food shops include **The Cheeseboard**, in the Westbury Centre off Grafton Street, for Irish farmhouse cheeses. Booksellers **Fred Hanna**, in Nassau Street, has a wide choice of Irish titles. For Irish music and instruments, go to **Walton's**, in North Frederick Street. Department stores are clustered round O'Connell and Henry Streets, north of the river. For atmosphere and barrow-boy backchat, visit the fruit and vegetable street market in Moore Street (daily except Sundays).

Shopping in Powerscourt Town House

NORTH AND WEST OF DUBLIN

WHAT TO SEE

◆◆◆
BRUGH NA BOINNE
west of Drogheda, off N51
This huge prehistoric graveyard in the valley of the Boyne is one of the largest concentrations of prehistoric structures in Ireland. The burial cairns, standing stones and earthworks were erected in what was then (around 5,000 years ago) heavily wooded countryside. The best known, first excavated in 1699, is **Newgrange**, some 300 feet (90m) across and around 36 feet (11m) high, made all the more eyecatching by its facing of white quartz stones along the river side. Some of the standing stones that once encircled it remain. A decorated threshold stone stands at the entrance, where a narrow passage leads to the central chamber. There are three burial alcoves here, and stones incised with abstract patterns. Unfortunately, Newgrange is too small to cope with the ever-increasing number of visitors; if you want to see it, avoid the summer months, especially weekends, or you may have to wait an hour or more for your guided tour.

Less accessible – some scrambling on all fours is needed to see it properly – is **Dowth** cairn, a couple of miles away. Check that it can be visited before setting off. The

Carving at Newgrange

third of the great cairns, **Knowth**, is still being excavated, but parts of the site, including several smaller satellite tombs, are now open to the public in summer.

◆◆◆
CASTLETOWN HOUSE
near Celbridge, off R403
This magnificent Georgian country mansion was built in the 1720s for the then richest man in Ireland, William Connolly, a Donegal innkeeper's son who rose to become Speaker of the Irish House of Commons. The spacious, elegant interior includes fine 18th-century furniture, portraits and superb plasterwork. From the window of the dramatic Long Gallery you can see a folly erected in the early 1740s to provide work at times of famine.

◆◆
CEANANNUS MÓR
Better known as Kells, this appealing town (pronounced 'kanannus more') was the site of a monastery founded in the 6th century by St Columcille (Columba). In around AD800 it produced the magnificent illuminated manuscript now known as the Book of Kells and held in Trinity College Library, Dublin. Interesting buildings include an attractive separate belfry beside the modern church, an early Christian church called St Columba's house, and a round tower. There are also five high crosses.

◆◆
COOLEY PENINSULA
Well worth a visit for unspoilt scenery of heather-covered hills and rock, the peninsula also offers views of the Mourne Mountains across Carlingford Lough. The village of **Carlingford** is attractive too, with its narrow lanes and little harbour. Several ancient ruins here include the 12th-century King John's Castle.

◆◆◆
MALAHIDE CASTLE
Malahide

The home of the Talbot family for nearly 800 years, the castle includes several memorable rooms from different periods, including the darkly panelled Jacobean Oak Room, the elegant 18th-century drawing rooms and the medieval great hall. Many of the walls are hung with fine portraits from the National Gallery's collection. Another good reason to visit Malahide is the Fry Model Railway, in adjacent buildings: its scale models demonstrate the history of Irish rail transport right up to the present, including Dublin's DART system.

◆◆
MONASTERBOICE
off N1, north of Drogheda

One of Ireland's finest and best-preserved high crosses, the Cross of Muiredach, stands here within the precincts of a ruined monastery. Close by are two more crosses (one also richly carved though more weathered), a monastic sundial, a 9th-century round tower and two small bare ruined churches.

◆◆
NEWBRIDGE HOUSE
Donabate

This Georgian mansion was built in 1737 for the Cobbe family who continued to live here until 1985. Rooms on view include the dining room, library and, grandest of all, the Red Drawing Room, all with fine plasterwork ceilings. Treasures of the house include fine Irish portraits, china and furniture. Rarest of all is the Museum of Curiosities, a delightful collection of curios and treasures built up by the family since the 1790s. The courtyard buildings have a display of coaches.

Malahide Castle

◆
SLANE
The four matching Georgian houses confronting each other across the main crossroads of this attractive village were reputedly built for four bickering sisters by their exasperated brother. On the outskirts, overlooking the River Boyne, is Slane Castle, a fine example of the Gothic revival style. Its splendid round ballroom with intricate plasterwork is one of several rooms now used for smart functions, but there are tours, on summer Sundays and bank holidays, a restaurant and even a nightclub. Rising above all this is the Hill of Slane, on which stand the remains of a 16th-century friary and college. On this hill, St Patrick is said to have lighted the first Paschal Fire in Ireland, symbolising the triumph of Christianity over paganism (prematurely).

◆
TRIM
On the edge of this attractive town, by the river, **King John's Castle** (1172) is the largest Anglo-Norman castle in Ireland, with a well-preserved south gate. Northeast of Trim are the ruins of **Bective Abbey**, founded for the Cistercians in 1150, and the **Hill of Tara**, the legendary site of the residence of the High Kings of Ireland.

Accommodation
Expensive:
Slane, Co Meath: **Beauparc** (T&C) (tel: (041) 24207) – home of the Earl of Mount Charles, who also owns Slane Castle; some bedrooms have a jacuzzi.

Medium:
Ardee, Co Louth: **The Gables** (GH) (tel: (041) 53789) – converted schoolhouse.
Ballymascanlon, near Dundalk, Co Louth: **Ballymascanlon House** 3-star (tel: (042) 71124) – Victorian country house hotel.
Drogheda, Co Louth: **Boyne Valley** 3-star (tel: (041) 37737) – converted country house just out of town.
Slane, Co Meath: **Conyngham Arms** 2-star. (tel: (041) 24155) – small, comfortable streetside hotel.

Cheap:
Duleek, Co Meath: **Annesbrook** (T&C) (tel: (041) 23293) – handsome mansion in private grounds, with log fires and home cooking.
Navan, Co Meath: **Balreask House** (FH) (tel: (046) 21155) – modern farmhouse two miles from town, off N3 from Dublin.

Restaurants
Medium:
Ardee, Co Louth: **The Gables** — see under **Accommodation**.
Collon, Co Louth: **Forge Gallery** (tel: (041) 26272) – attractively furnished restaurant; dinner only.
Skerries, Co Dublin: **Red Bank**, 7 Church Street (tel: (01) 491005) – relaxed, intimate family-run restaurant in converted bank, specialising in seafood; dinner only.

Cheap:
Dundalk, Co Louth: **Cellars** (tel: (042) 33745) – good home cooking with vegetarian bias; lunch weekdays only, dinner Thursday to Saturday.

SOUTH OF DUBLIN

WHAT TO SEE

◆
ABBEYLEIX HOUSE GARDENS
Abbeyleix

A few miles inside County Laois, over the border with Co Kilkenny, this Georgian mansion (1773) is set in attractive grounds, with an ancient oak wood and a monastic bridge. The estate was the work of the first Viscount de Vesci, also responsible for the pleasant town of Abbeyleix.

◆
AVOCA HANDWEAVERS CENTRE
Avoca

Set in wooded countryside whose beauty inspired Thomas Moore's poem *The Meeting of the Waters* (1807), the centre includes the old mill, a weaving shed where you can watch handweavers at work, and a well-stocked shop and tearoom.

◆◆◆
GLENDALOUGH

A mountain valley with two lakes flanked by wooded hills is the setting for one of Ireland's most important early Christian sites. According to the legends, St Kevin fled here to escape the temptations of the flesh, and slept in a cave in a rock face overlooking the Upper Lake. A monastery grew up around him, and became a renowned centre of learning until it was burned and abandoned in 1398. The main part of the site is near the Lower Lake. The monastery gateway, the only surviving example in Ireland, leads into a large graveyard of old and new gravestones, trees and shrubs, in which stand several ruined buildings. The largest of these is the **cathedral**, built in the 11th and 12th centuries. Other buildings include a near-

Glendalough's upper lake is set in the Wicklow Mountains

The evocative nave and chancel of Jerpoint Abbey

perfect round tower; an oratory called **St Kevin's Kitchen** and a church with fine Irish Romanesque decoration. Near the Upper Lake, which can be reached by a pleasant woodland walk or by road, are the foundations of a beehive cell, and the ruins of a church and a prehistoric stone fort. There is an excellent interpretive centre. Glendalough attracts many thousands of visitors a year, and both crowds and litter detract from its atmosphere, so visit it off-season if you can.

◆◆
IRISH NATIONAL HERITAGE PARK
Ferrycarrig
This makes a good introduction to the prehistoric and ancient history of Ireland up to medieval times. The open-air display consists of replicas of representative structures, starting with an early Stone Age 'campsite' and finishing at a round tower, with explanations of the social context. There is also a visitors' centre, with an audio-visual show.

◆◆◆
JERPOINT ABBEY
near Thomastown
One of Ireland's most beautiful and complete ruined abbeys. Founded by the Cistercians in 1180, the church and monastic buildings are ranged along three sides of a 15th-century cloister (rebuilt in 1953) which is decorated with some delightful carved stone panels. The oldest parts of the church are the chancel and transepts, both good examples of Irish Romanesque. The church contains a number of fine tombs including that of the first abbot, Felix O'Dullany.

◆
JOHNSTOWN CASTLE ESTATE
near Wexford

The Gothic-revival castle itself is not open, but the landscaped grounds include three ornamental lakes and are very attractive. Outbuildings house the Irish Agricultural Museum: its extensive displays illustrate rural domestic life and crafts, with reconstructions of typical interiors and a fine collection of Irish country furniture.

◆◆
KELLS

Not the Kells whence came the Book of Kells (see Ceanannus Mór), but an important ancient ecclesiastical site all the same, as it is the largest monastic enclosure in Ireland. Its Norman founder, Geoffrey Fitzrobert, saw to it that the Augustinian monks were well defended; as well as walls and rampart towers, there was a moat between the monastic buildings and the rest of the settlement, which was probably used as a cattle pound.

Access still requires some agility.

◆
JOHN F KENNEDY PARK
near Dunganstown

Dunganstown was the site of the Kennedy family's ancestral home. The park is just south, an extensive arboretum with some 4,500 varieties of trees and shrubs. There is also a lake, and, in the main season, a pony and trap service.

◆
KILCOOLEY ABBEY
Kilcooley

On the other side of the Slieveardagh Mountains from Kilkenny, this Cistercian abbey was founded in 1182 but much rebuilt after its destruction in 1445. The ruins include a fine east window and good carved stonework, including the early 16th-century tomb of Piers Fitz Oge Butler.

◆
KILDARE

The town's history stretches back to the 5th or 6th century, to the foundation of a nunnery by St Brigid. Its oldest remaining monument is a 100-foot (30m) round tower, probably 12th-century, with a Romanesque doorway. The cathedral was built in the 13th century on the site of several older churches; parts of the original structure survive, though the church was heavily, albeit accurately, restored by G E Street in the 1870s. It contains several interesting medieval monuments.

◆◆◆
KILKENNY

Once a rival to Dublin as the seat of government, Kilkenny flourished in the 14th to 17th centuries, leaving a fine heritage of medieval and Tudor buildings. These combine with its winding streets and its setting on the banks of the River Nore to make it a delightful town. Kilkenny holds its own festival in late August. **St Canice's**

Cathedral stands in the northern part of the city, known as Irishtown because the native Irish settled there when driven out of the Old Town by the 14th-century Statute of Kilkenny.

Most of the cathedral's fabric dates from the 13th century, restored in the 1860s, and it contains many fine tombstones. A short walk away stands the **Black Abbey**, a Dominican friary church incorporating parts of the medieval structure. The city's other imposing medieval building is the **castle**, best seen from John's Bridge. Despite its convincing appearance, only three of the huge towers and parts of the curtain walls are original 13th-century work; the rest is largely early 19th-century remodelling, though there is a fine 1685 gateway. The castle stables, opposite, house the **Kilkenny Design Workshops**, where a range of craft items are made.

◆
KILMORE QUAY
The main street of this unspoilt fishing village, with several thatched cottages, runs down to the working harbour where a restored lightship has been converted into a little maritime museum. Exhibits include a collection of newspaper cuttings about the village.

◆◆
KILRUDDERY HOUSE
near Bray
South of the popular resort of Bray, with its mile-long esplanade, amusement arcades and guesthouses, Kilruddery is the elegant home of Lord and Lady Meath whose estate includes the Sugar Loaf. Much of the house is early 19th-century Elizabethan style: a large older part succumbed to dry rot in the 1950s, though fortunately the original 1680s library survives, with wood carving by Grinling Gibbons. Other rooms on show include the living room, with fine furniture and good plasterwork, and a large conservatory. Another survivor of the 17th century is the garden, laid out with canals, hedges and statuary.

Kilkenny castle and park

The view from Powerscourt

◆◆
MOUNT USHER GARDENS
near Ashford
Laid out in 1868, the 20 or so acres (8 hectares) form a collection of rare and exotic plants and trees, including 70 species of eucalyptus. Winding paths and little bridges across a stream make a romantic setting.

◆◆◆
POWERSCOURT ESTATE
Ireland's best-known gardens lie just outside the pleasant village of Enniskerry. At their centre stands the melancholy shell of a handsome 18th-century mansion gutted by fire in the 1970s, which may yet be restored. The gardens, laid out in the Victorian era, celebrate several styles. Dropping away from the back of the mansion towards a small lake are the broad terraces of the formal Italian Garden, looking across to the Great Sugar Loaf mountain. There are also Japanese gardens, walled gardens and herbaceous borders, superb trees and a fine collection of decorative features, including statuary and wrought-iron work. There is also a children's play area, a tearoom, a shop and a garden centre. Some four miles (6.5km) away is Powerscourt Waterfall, the highest in Ireland.

◆◆
RUSSBOROUGH HOUSE
near Blessington
This handsome granite Palladian mansion was built in the early 18th century for Joseph Leeson, who gave his

name to Dublin's Leeson Street and Park. Bought by Sir Alfred Beit, it now houses his fine art collection, including works by masters of the 17th-century Dutch and Spanish schools, though a robbery in 1986 deprived it of some of its most valuable paintings. The elegant interior is also furnished with superb plasterwork by the Swiss-Italian Lafranchini brothers, besides marble mantelpieces, bronzes and porcelain, 18th-century tapestries and Louis XVI furniture.

◆
ST MULLINS
The wooded valley of the River Barrow is a peaceful setting for a collection of medieval buildings including an abbey church named after the 7th-century Saint Moling, and the base of a round tower. The graveyard bristles with crosses and headstones, and a stone shrine sheltering metal banners carrying the names of men killed in the 1798 rebellion. The steep little hill near by is a Norman castle mound.

◆◆
TULLY HOUSE
near Kildare
Home of the National Stud and Irish Horse Museum, which includes the skeleton of the great 1960s champion, Arkle, Tully House is also known for its delightful little Japanese Garden. The garden was laid out in 1906–10 to a design symbolising the stages of human life from birth to eternal life.

◆
WEXFORD
Wexford's main attraction for visitors is its prestigious autumn Opera Festival, with productions staged in the town's delightful 19th-century theatre. Otherwise the town has little to show for its long history, apart from the medieval West Gate, and remnants of the town walls. The town suffered at the hands of Oliver Cromwell and again in the 1798 rising, commemorated by a statue in the Bullring. Another statue, in Crescent Quay overlooking the harbour, is of John Barry, local-born founder of the American navy.

Accommodation
Expensive:
Gorey, Co Wexford: **Marlfield House** 3-star (tel: (055) 21124) – Regency country house, with excellent restaurant.
Rathnew, Co Wicklow: **Tinakilly House** 3-star (tel: (0404) 69274) – Victorian Italianate mansion, with good restaurant.

Medium:
Kilkenny, Co Kilkenny: **Newpark** 3-star, Castlecomer Road (tel: (056) 22122) – converted old house with modern extensions in parkland, next to golf course.
Prosperous, Naas, Co Kildare: **Curryhills House** 2-star (tel: (045) 68150) – extended Georgian farmhouse, with good restaurant.
Rathnew, Co Wicklow: **Hunter's** 2-star (tel: (0404) 40106) – family-run coaching inn with riverside garden; nice

place for tea, also good restaurant.

Rosslare, Co Wexford: **Kelly's Strand** 3-star (tel: (053) 32114) – large hotel with extensive facilities, geared towards families and enthusiastically run by the Kellys.

Cheap:

Dunbell, Maddockstown, Co Kilkenny: **Blanchville House** (FH) (tel: (056) 27197) – Georgian house on a working farm.

Kilgreaney, Muine Bheag (Bagenalstown), Co Carlow: **Lorum Old Rectory** (T&C) (tel: (0503) 75282) – comfortable old house run with skill and relaxed style, good home cooking.

Rathdrum, Co Wicklow: **Avonbrae** (GH) (tel: (0404) 46198) – beautiful setting, with indoor heated pool.

The Rower, Co Kilkenny: **Cullintra House** (T&C) (tel: (051) 23614) – attractive 18th-century farmhouse in wooded countryside, run in highly individualistic style. Also **Garranavabby House** (FH) (tel: (051) 23613) – large, old creeper-clad family house with charming rooms and welcoming owner.

Restaurants
Expensive:

Gorey, Co Wexford: **Marlfield House** — see under **Accommodation**.

Medium:

Bray, Co Wicklow: **Tree of Idleness**, Seafront (tel: (01) 863498) – rare chance to feast on Greek/Cypriot cooking, re-interpreted in modern style, in

much-lauded family-run restaurant; dinner only.

Castledermot, Co Kildare: **Doyle's Schoolhouse** (tel: (0503) 44282) – comfortable restaurant with friendly chef-proprietor; modern-style cooking, mainly dinners and good-value Sunday lunches. Also B&B.

Dunlavin, Co Wicklow: **Rathsallagh House** (tel: (045) 53112) – rambling country house restaurant and hotel in beautiful countryside, popular with horseracing and country sports crowd; hearty dinners of local produce, and extended Sunday lunches.

Kilkenny, Co Kilkenny: **Lacken House**, Dublin Road (tel: (056) 65611) – inventive modern cooking by chef-patron Eugene Sweeney; dinner only, also B&B.

Rathnew, Co Wicklow: **Hunter's** — see under **Accommodation**.

Cheap:

Ballyhack, near New Ross, Co Wexford: **Neptune** (tel: (051) 89284) – small, owner-run riverside restaurant, specialising in seafood.

Blessington, Co Wicklow: **The Courtyard, Tulfarris House** (tel: (045) 64574) – converted coach buildings, serving simple bistro-style meals all day.

Kilkenny, Co Kilkenny: **Edward Langton** (tel: (056) 21728) – award-winning bar food, attractive interior.

Leighlinbridge, Co Carlow: **Lord Bagenal Inn** (tel: (0503) 21668) – modern riverside pub serving bar lunches, snacks and evening meals.

CORK AND THE SOUTH
CORK

Cork has never really accepted Dublin's supremacy. It may be second to the capital in size, but it too is a lively metropolis which can claim as long and rich a history as its rival. Unfortunately, Cork was on the losing side in a number of past political conflicts, one reason why little has survived of its medieval and Georgian buildings. Today there are signs of dereliction and decay in some areas, but even so the city's overall atmosphere is one of vigour and confidence. An 18th-century visitor would have seen huge ocean-going vessels berthed in the city's heart, in what are now Patrick Street and Grand Parade. Although all but two main channels of the river have been covered over, central Cork remains a waterside city connected by bridges. Cork has more traffic than it can cope with, plus a one-way system and ring-roads. The river has two arms, so beware relying on the sight of water to orientate yourself. If given directions that refer to 'The Statue', this means the figure of Father Theobald Mathew, fervent exponent of temperance, that stands at the end of Patrick Street facing St Patrick's Bridge. You will need a disc for street parking – there are four zones, each with different hourly limits – and finding a space in the centre can be difficult. There is a large municipal car park in Lavitt's Quay.

WHAT TO SEE IN THE CITY CENTRE

◆◆
CRAWFORD MUNICIPAL ART GALLERY
Emmet Place
Housed in what was once the Georgian Custom House, later extended and turned into an art school, the gallery's permanent displays include works by 19th- and 20th-century Irish artists including Lavery, Orpen and Yeats, and their English contemporaries; paintings by 18th-century Cork-born James Barry; a sculpture gallery; and stained glass by Harry Clarke (1889–1931). The gallery also hosts temporary exhibitions. Its restaurant is one of the best in Cork.

◆
ST ANN'S CHURCH, SHANDON
Church Street
An 18th-century replacement of a medieval church, St Ann's has an eyecatching two-tone tower – half red sandstone, half white limestone – and a peal of eight bells, which visitors are allowed to ring for a small fee.

◆◆◆
ST FIN BARRE'S CATHEDRAL
Bishop Street
A characteristically uninhibited design by that exuberant exponent of Gothic revival, William Burges. Built in the 1870s, it was the third cathedral on this site. Its interior is a bit of a disappointment after the rich detail of the outside.

CORK AND THE SOUTH

WHAT TO SEE BEYOND THE CITY CENTRE

◆◆
CORK PUBLIC MUSEUM
Fitzgerald Park
The city's museum is housed in a Georgian mansion in an attractive park a short walk west along Mardyke Walk. The collections include displays on Cork's lace and glass industries and merchant banks.

◆◆
DUNKATHEL HOUSE
Glanmire
Dunkathel is a Georgian mansion, built in about 1790, with a fine interior. Features include a 19th-century painted hallway, a handsome Bath stone staircase and Adam fireplaces. As well as Irish antique furniture, there is a collection of Victorian watercolours and a Victorian barrel organ.

◆◆
RIVERSIDE HOUSE
Glanmire
Dating from 1602, the house was done up in the 1730s by its owner, Jemmett Browne, who later became Archbishop of Cork. He employed the best plaster artists, the Lafranchini brothers, then newly arrived in Ireland, whose glorious designs adorn the dining room ceiling and walls. Rescued in the 1960s after a period of decay, the house is now fully restored.

Accommodation
Cork's best hotels are in suburbs, mainly to the east.

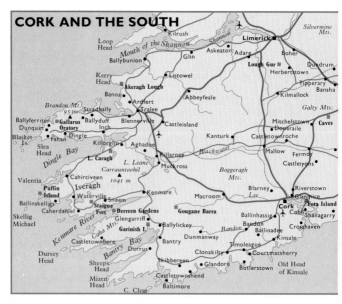

Expensive:
Jury's 4-star, Western Road
(tel: (021) 276622) – a short
walk west from the centre;
large, modern, with good
sports facilities.
Fitzpatrick Silver Springs
3-star, Lower Glanmire Road
(N25), Tivoli (tel: (021) 507533) –
large and modern, with a nine
hole golf course, tennis and
squash courts and a pool.

Medium:
Arbutus Lodge, Middle
Glanmire Road, Mottenotte (tel:
(021) 501237) – small family-run
hotel in an extended 1802
townhouse, with a fine
collection of modern Irish art
and an acclaimed restaurant.
Ashbourne House,
Glounthaune (tel: (021) 353319)
– another early 19th-century
house, set back off the N25 in
extensive gardens overlooking
the River Lee.
Lotamore House (GH), Tivoli
(tel: (021) 822344) – Georgian
manor beside N25, with well-
equipped rooms; no restaurant
but snacks and cold meals
available.

Cheap:
Antoine House (T&C), Western
Road (tel: (021) 543289) – small
guesthouse, close to the
University. There is also an **An
Oige** youth hostel in Western
Road (tel: (021) 432891).

Restaurants
Expensive:
Arbutus Lodge — see under
Accommodation.

*St Fin Barre's Victorian exuberance
is reflected in the River Lee*

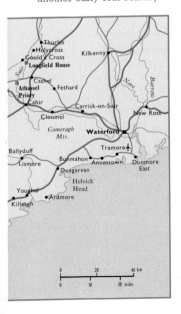

One of Patrick Street's sights

Clifford's, 18 Dyke Parade (tel: (021) 275333) – first-class cooking of traditional dishes combined with modern presentation.

Medium:

Crawford Gallery Café, Emmet Place (tel: (021) 274415) – serves delicious lunches and snacks, also dinner on Wednesday to Friday evenings.

O'Keeffe's, 23 Washington Street West (tel: (021) 275645) – small restaurant with emphasis on seafood.

Cheap:

Periwinkle, Queens Oldcastle Shopping Centre (tel: (021) 271199) – seafood bar.

Quay Co-op, 24 Sullivan's Quay (tel: (021) 967660) – wholefood restaurant.

Entertainment

For information about what's on, ask at the tourist office or get the *Cork Examiner* or the *Evening Echo*. Both carry daily listings of theatre and films.

Shopping

Patrick Street is the main shopping thoroughfare; and there are several interesting shops, in the pedestrianised Carey's Lane/French Church Street/Paul Street district. Try **Crafts of Ireland**, in Winthrop Street, and **The House of James**, in Paul Street. Near St Ann's, in the old Butter Exchange, is the small **Shandon Crafts Centre**. The 'English Market', in the city centre, is a lively covered food market.

EAST AND NORTH OF CORK

WHAT TO SEE

◆◆
ADARE

This picturesque showpiece village owes much of its genteel appearance to an early 19th-century Earl of Dunraven who 'improved' it with a wide main street flanked by thatched and slate-roofed cottages. Older buildings include an Augustinian priory, close to the medieval 14-arch bridge, and a Trinitarian friary, now the Catholic church. Both were restored from ruinous state by the improving Earl. His family seat, Adare Manor, is now one of Ireland's most luxurious hotels, and hosts an impressive annual international festival of music and drama in July.

◆◆
ANNESGROVE GARDENS
Castletownroche
The romantic riverside gardens which surround an 18th-century house include woodland walks, a cliff garden overlooking a lily pond, a walled garden, herbaceous borders and many fine shrubs including rare rhododendron species.

◆
ARDMORE

Rising up from the attractive, well-kept village is one of the best-preserved round towers in Ireland. It stands amid a collection of early Christian buildings including a small cathedral with some unusual Romanesque sculptures.

◆◆
BLARNEY CASTLE
Blarney
The castle's Stone of Eloquence pulls in the crowds: it is said to impart fluent speech – but once visitors have climbed the steps up to it many have little breath left to test their newly acquired power. Even if the hype makes you suspicious, the castle itself is worth a visit – a fine 15th-century keep set in attractive riverside gardens which include a late 18th-century rock garden. The ramparts give a good view of Blarney Castle House, open in summer.

◆◆
CAHIR CASTLE
Cahir
On a rocky island in the River Suir, the large medieval castle is one of the best-preserved in Ireland, though helped by restoration work in the 1840s. The attractive town has some Georgian buildings beside a pleasant riverside walk.

◆
CARRICK-ON-SUIR MANOR HOUSE
Carrick-on-Suir
In front of a ruined castle stands the finest Elizabethan manor house in Ireland, containing some superb original plasterwork. The town, with winding narrow streets, is attractively sited on the banks of the River Suir.

◆◆◆
CASHEL

Rising 300 feet (90m) from the plain of the Golden Vale, the **Rock of Cashel** has been the centre of attention hereabouts for some 1,600 years. The stronghold of Munster's kings from the 4th to 12th centuries, it took on great spiritual significance after a visit by St Patrick in the 5th century. The group of ruins on its summit includes the fine 12th-century Cormac's Chapel, with abundant Romanesque decoration; a complete round tower, possibly 11th-century; the roofless cathedral with a soaring crossing and carved tombs; a 15th-century archbishops' castle; and the restored Hall of the Vicars Choral, displaying copies of medieval artefacts and furniture. Stone sculptures include the original, much-weathered 12th-century high cross, replaced outside by a replica.

In fields below the Rock lie the ruins of **Hore Abbey**, a 13th-century Cistercian foundation. The town itself is also full of interest. **St John the Baptist Cathedral** was built in the Classical style in the late 18th to early 19th century; next to it, the **GPA Bolton Library** (1836) exhibits some of its fine collection of over 11,000 items, including illuminated manuscripts and early printed books.

Earlier buildings include the handsome **Cashel Palace Hotel** built in about 1730 as the bishop's palace; a 15th-century tower; and the remains of a friary, **St Dominick's**.

A **Folk Village**, in Dominic Street, is an interesting little collection of small outbuildings kitted out as a kitchen, pub and so on, with a Republican museum.

Cashel's cathedral and castle stand firm on the rock

◆◆
CLONMEL

This characterful riverside market town was the birthplace of that 18th-century original, the novelist Laurence Sterne. Some of the buildings he must have known still survive, including the 17th-century assizes court, Main Guard, its arcade now enclosed by shops. There are several Georgian buildings, including the fine Classical courthouse (1802). The town museum, together with a gallery, is in Parnell Street. Clonmel is famous for its greyhounds – three appear on the town arms, and there is a race track. The surrounding district is also known for racehorse breeding.

◆◆
COBH

A delightful seaside town with a predominantly Regency and early Victorian character, Cobh (pronounced 'Cove') began to grow during the Napoleonic Wars, thanks to its position on a fine natural harbour. Streets and terraces climb the hill from the waterfront up to the town's dominant building, Augustus Pugin's Gothic revival cathedral, St Colman's. For many Irish emigrants, Cobh was their last contact with Irish soil before they embarked on their desperate and too often fatal journeys to the New World. Cobh was also the last resting place for many of the victims of the *Lusitania* disaster in 1915, one of the subjects covered by the little

maritime museum housed in a converted church. In July, Cobh attracts many visitors to its International Folk Dance Festival.

◆◆
FOTA ISLAND

Fota House and its estate take up much of this sheltered island, whose mild climate allows many temperate and subtropical species of tree and shrub to flourish in a fine arboretum. The house itself is an early 18th-century hunting lodge transformed in the 1820s by architect Richard Morrison into a superb Regency mansion. It provides an elegant setting for an extensive collection of Irish landscape paintings of the 1750s to 1870s. Part of the estate is now a wildlife park, with many endangered species. The island is reached by a causeway.

◆◆
HOLYCROSS ABBEY
Holycross

Once a major place of pilgrimage – it still displays its relic of the True Cross – this splendid example of 15th-century architecture was recently restored after years of decay. One rare feature is a wall painting of a hunting scene.

◆◆◆
LIMERICK

The third largest city in the Republic, Limerick was founded by Viking settlers on the banks of the River Shannon. It is now a bustling commercial and industrial centre, boosted by its proximity to Shannon International Airport. The oldest surviving building, **St Mary's Cathedral**, was founded at the end of the 12th century; the choir contains some delightful 15th-century misericords (carvings beneath the choir stall seats – the only ones in Ireland) and there are some fine tombs. In summer, the cathedral provides the setting for a nightly *son et lumière* show. Its near contemporary, **King John's Castle** has recently been restored.

Parts of the castle walls bear witness to the destruction suffered by Limerick in 1691, during a prolonged siege by the troops of William III. Despite valiant resistance, the city eventually capitulated, and a treaty was signed, supposedly on the **Treaty Stone** which stands on the west side of Thomond Bridge. Though Limerick is a busy modern city, its centre includes districts with a distinctive Georgian elegance. These include Pery Square, overlooking the People's Park, in which stands the **City Art Gallery**, with its collection of 18th- to 20th-century Irish art. Another Georgian area is John Square, which includes the **City Museum**. The **Belltable Arts Centre**, which stages art exhibitions and theatre performances, is in the wide main thoroughfare, O'Connell Street, which also has some handsome Georgian doorways. Apart from the Treaty, and the comic verse form supposedly invented in a city pub, the name of Limerick is associated with lace, still being made in Clare Street by the Good Shepherd Sisters (the gateway sign says Mary Crest).

On the outskirts, at the University of Limerick at

St Mary's Cathedral, Limerick

Plassey, is the **Hunt Collection**, whose treasures include Celtic and medieval antiquities and works of art, both Irish and European, as well as Limoges enamels and Georgian silver.

◆◆
LOUGH GUR
near Herbertstown
The horseshoe lake is at the centre of an area crowded with Stone Age and early Christian monuments. A visitors' centre has an audio-visual show and displays, and runs walking tours. One of the stone circles, near the Limerick road, is the largest in Ireland.

◆◆
MITCHELSTOWN CAVES
near Mitchelstown
A half-mile-long show cave can be visited here, including spectacular rock formations. The caves were discovered in 1833.

◆
WATERFORD
Few Irish cities are so strongly identified with a single product as Waterford. Its manufacture of fine cut glass dates back to the 16th century, though heavy taxes crushed the industry for nearly a century until it was revived in 1947. The modern factory, southwest of the centre off the Cork road, is open to visitors (no children allowed on factory tour). In the town, most of the sights are situated within a small area on or close to the quay. The city has two theatres, and hosts a 16-night Festival of Light Opera in September, for competing amateur operatic societies from Ireland and abroad, with many fringe events.

◆◆
YOUGHAL
The first potatoes in Ireland are said to have been planted by Sir Walter Raleigh in the grounds of his Youghal home Myrtle Grove, an event celebrated annually by the town's 10-day Walter Raleigh Potato Festival, in late June/early July. Raleigh was given this delightful seaside town (pronounced 'Yawl') as a gift by his grateful monarch. Its finest building is St Mary's Collegiate Church, dating from the 13th century, which contains several superb monuments, most sumptuous of all the 1619 wall monument of Richard Boyle, Earl of Cork, and his family. Near by are well-preserved remains of the town walls. In the main street is the attractive Clock Gate (1777). The town's long, safe sandy beach, with amusement arcades, lies to the west of town, towards Knockadoon Head.

Accommodation
Expensive:
Adare, Co Tipperary:
Dunraven Arms 3-star (tel: (061) 396209) – comfortable, antique-furnished.
Cashel, Co Tipperary:
Cashel Palace 4-star (tel: (062) 61411) – Queen Anne mansion, once a bishop's palace.
Mallow, Co Cork: **Longueville House** 3-star (tel: (022) 47156) – Georgian mansion beside the Blackwater River, with highly regarded restaurant.

Waterford, Co Waterford: **Waterford Castle** 3-star, The Island, Ballinakill (tel: (051) 78203) – luxuriously converted Norman castle on an island, which is reached by free car ferry.

Medium:
Castlelyons, Co Cork: **Ballyvolane** (T&C) (tel: (025) 36349) – comfortable Victorian house in extensive private grounds.
Clonmel, Co Tipperary: **Knocklofty House**, on Ardfinnan road (tel: (052) 38222) – large Georgian mansion in extensive grounds beside River Suir, with leisure centre; also beside the river, **Minella** 3-star (tel: (052) 22388) – Georgian house with modern extensions.
Dunmore East, Co Waterford: **Haven** 2-star (tel: (051) 83150) – small hotel in own grounds, with sea views.
Kanturk, Co Cork: **Assolas Country House** (GH) (tel: (029) 50015) – delightful 17th-century house in idyllic riverside setting, with good restaurant.
Shanagarry, Co Cork: **Ballymaloe House** (GH) (tel: (021) 652531) – the Allen family's highly praised country house hotel, part of it converted from a 14th-century castle, with outstanding restaurant.

Cheap:
Bansha, Co Tipperary: **Bansha House** (FH) (tel: (062) 54194) – Georgian farmhouse close to Galtee Mountains.
Killeagh, Co Cork: **Ballymakeigh House** (FH) (tel: (024) 95184) – exceptional

cooking, relaxed and welcoming atmosphere; facilities include games room and tennis court.
Waterford, Co Waterford: **Blenheim House**, Ballymaclode (tel: (051) 74115) – antique-furnished Georgian home near to Passage East car ferry.

Restaurants
Expensive:
Mallow, Co Cork: **Longueville House** — see under **Accommodation**.

Medium:
Adare, Co Limerick: **Mustard Seed** (tel: (061) 86451) – skilful, sophisticated cooking in charming cottage setting; dinner only.
Cashel, Co Tipperary: **Chez Hans** (tel: (062) 61177) – well-established French restaurant in converted church; dinner only.
Shanagarry, Co Cork: **Ballymaloe House** – see under **Accommodation**.
Waterford, Co Waterford: **Dwyers** (tel: (051) 77478) – mainly French provincial style cooking; dinner only.
Youghal, Co Cork: **Aherne's Seafood Bar** (tel: (024) 92424) – fresh seafood forms the basis of good-value bar meals and the rather grander restaurant menu.

Cheap:
Clonmel, Co Tipperary: **Abbey Co-op** (tel: (052) 21457) – wholefood café, for lunches and daytime snacks.
Dunmore East, Co Waterford: **The Ship** (tel: (051) 83141) – attractive pub with interesting, mainly fish dishes.

Bantry House's fine interior

WEST OF CORK

Generations of travellers have sung the praises of the southwest corner of Ireland. Its beauty is of the ravishing, hit-you-between-the-eyes sort – dramatic ragged peninsulas, with mountains dropping down into the wild Atlantic, and, inland, great stretches of unspoilt moorland. The main sights can get crowded in high season but, even so, it is always possible to find peace and isolation, particularly if you head inland from the sea.

◆ ARDFERT

Several interesting ruins here include the roofless remains of a cathedral dating from the 13th century, with a couple of fine wall effigies. Beside it are a Romanesque and a 15th-century church; and, a short walk away in the grounds of Ardfert House, a ruined Franciscan friary.

◆◆◆ BANTRY HOUSE

Bantry

In a superb setting overlooking the bay, this exquisite stately home is richly furnished with antiques, portraits, tapestries and china, much of it collected by Richard White, 2nd Earl of Bantry, whose descendants still own and live in the house. Part early 18th-century, with Georgian and mid-Victorian extensions, its rooms on view include the spectacular dining room, with richly carved furniture and gilded picture frames set against royal-blue walls; the delicate Rose Drawing Room, with its 17th-century Aubusson tapestries; the Gobelins Drawing Room; and the large library, overlooking the Italianate gardens. The wings of the house have been elegantly converted into guest accommodation.

◆
BLENNERVILLE WINDMILL CENTRE
Blennerville

The restored windmill is a relic of the village's history as an important 18th- to 19th-century port, until bypassed by the nearby Tralee Ship Canal. Displays in the adjacent visitors' centre include an Emigration Exhibition, and there are several craft studios, a gift shop and a café. Nearby **Tralee** holds a week-long festival each year, centred on an international beauty contest for the 'Rose of Tralee'. It is also home to the National Folk Theatre of Ireland, Siamsa Tíre, with performances combining traditional dance, music and singing.

◆
CASTLETOWNSHEND

Set on a steep hill dropping to a sheltered harbour, this attractive Georgian village was home to a number of well-to-do families in the 19th century. They included that of the writer Edith Somerville (1858–1949), best known for her novel *Some Experiences of an Irish RM* and its sequel, written in collaboration with Violet Martin (who used the pen-name Ross). The two friends are buried in the village churchyard. Halfway up the main street is Mary Ann's, a singing pub. For marvellous views of the coast to the west, take the forest

Castletownshend

park leading up from Lough Hyne, southwest of the village, off the Baltimore road.

◆
CLONAKILTY

A pleasant market town with an old-fashioned charm, Clonakilty lies close to several sandy beaches. A converted brewery houses the West Cork Craft and Design Centre and gallery, selling work by some 180 craftspeople. Pearse Street has the friendly, traditional-style O'Donovan's Hotel and pub; De Barra, a music pub; and a butcher's, Edward Twomey, known throughout Ireland for its black pudding. A 10-day West Cork Festival is held at the end of June.

◆◆
CRAG CAVE
Castleisland
Crag Cave is actually an extensive underground complex of caves, not explored and mapped until the 1980s. The tour includes two vast chambers, and many dramatic limestone formations.

◆◆
DERREEN GARDENS
Lauragh
Set in an area known for its wild rhododendrons, the sub-tropical gardens have not only many cultivated rhododendron species, but also camellias, tree ferns, bamboos and a collection of fine trees, including giant conifers planted in the 1880s. To the south, a mountain road rises up past Glanmore Lough through the fine scenery of the Beara Peninsula – a good area for ridge walking.

◆
DERRYNANE HOUSE
Caherdaniel
This was the family home of one of Ireland's most famous sons, Daniel O'Connell (1775–1847), nicknamed 'The Liberator' for his successful non-violent campaign for Catholic emancipation. The house, much altered by O'Connell after he inherited it in 1825, is now a museum. The estate includes several sheltered beaches; the longest is unsafe for swimming but has a nature trail through the sand dunes.

◆◆◆
DINGLE PENINSULA
A wild, beautiful peninsula, Dingle is also remarkable for its prehistoric and early Christian monuments. It has around 2,000 in all, including standing stones, ring forts, beehive huts and crosses. One of the best-preserved and most accessible is the **Gallarus Oratory**, an unmortared stone building, shaped like an upturned boat, which remains weather-tight after 12 centuries. A particularly large cluster of ancient remains can be seen in the area of **Fahan**, near Slea Head; rumour has it that enterprising local farmers, who are likely to charge you for entering their fields, have helped to boost the number. Wonderful views (weather permitting) are to be had from **Slea Head**; from **Brandon Mountain** (where saintly powers of sight gave St Brendan a vision of the Island of the Blessed); and from the

Cloud break over the Three Sisters

road from Dingle to Tralee, through the **Conor Pass**. Bicycling is a good way to enjoy the coast route; there's a rental office in **Dingle**, a pleasant, lively resort and fishing centre with a number of craft shops and good restaurants. Off the peninsula lie the **Blasket Islands**, whose last residents left in 1954; accounts of their way of life include *The Islandman* by Tomás O Criomhthain, and Flann O'Brien's sly, surreal antidote to nostalgic Irishry, *The Poor Mouth*. Boat trips to the islands can be made in spring and summer, weather permitting, from Dunquin, a village used for the filming of *Ryan's Daughter*. The peninsula has several good beaches, including the long spit of Inch Strand, Stradbally Strand, Ballyquin and Smerwick Harbour. Gaelic is still widely spoken on the Dingle, and the area's literature and archaeology are covered by a heritage centre at **Ballyferriter**.

◆◆
GARINISH ISLAND
Glengarriff Harbour
A triumph of horticulture over nature, this island was transformed from what was bare rock in 1910 into an exotic paradise of sub-tropical vegetation. The island is reached by private boats, which are not cheap. Visitors should ask the local tourist office for names of approved operators. The resort of Glengarriff, sheltered by the mountains and nestling in a lush landscape of arbutus, fuchsia, holly and yew, is a popular centre for swimming, fishing and boating.

◆
KENMARE

Laid out in the 1770s by the Marquess of Lansdowne, this charming, mainly 19th-century town is a good centre for touring the Beara and Iveragh peninsulas. The area also offers fine salmon fishing and walking: to the southwest are the Cloonee and Inchiquin lakes, set in ancient woodlands, and there are exhilarating ridge walks in Macgillycuddy's Reeks, to the north. The road from Glengariff through Kenmare to Killarney passes through spectacular scenery.

◆◆◆
KILLARNEY VALLEY

The dramatic, romantic scenery has been attracting tourists to this part of Ireland since the 18th century. Without it, few would find reason to visit, let alone stay in, Killarney itself. Its only building of note is **St Mary's Cathedral** (1840s), designed by Pugin. The **National Museum of Irish Transport**, in Scotts Hotel Gardens, has a collection of vintage cars, cycles, carriages and the like. There are race meetings in summer, and a particularly attractive, top-quality golf course.

The town's most immediate scenic asset is **Lough Leane** which, with Middle and Upper Lakes, can be explored on a day's boat trip. On dry land, the best views of the lakes are from Aghadoe, at the north end, and Lady's View, near the south end. Of the 40 or so islands, **Inisfallen** was for over 1,000 years the site of an important monastery; all that now remains is the ruin of a 12th-century Augustinian friary and a small Romanesque church. Boat trips leave from the quay beside **Ross Castle**, a 16th-century tower next to a 17th-century house.

Another popular summer excursion is by pony or pony trap (jaunting car) through the seven mile (11km) **Gap of Dunloe**, a dramatic glacial ravine. Round tours from Killarney follow this with a boat trip back up through the lakes to Ross Castle.

Lough Leane from the gardens of Muckross House

◆◆◆
KINSALE

Lively without being brash, this seaside village rising up from a sheltered harbour has bags of charm, though not of a particularly Irish sort. A network of lanes, a colourful waterfront, and the attractive old buildings, many hung with slate, all encourage gentle promenades. For the more active, there is sailing, scuba diving and fishing. The local museum is housed in a 17th-century courthouse; other buildings of note are St Multose Church, parts of which are late 12th-century; and a town house, Desmond Castle, also called the French Prison because of its use during the Napoleonic Wars. Kinsale also has an extraordinary number of restaurants, and in October holds a Gourmet Festival. Outside the town, next to the pretty village of Summer Cove, is the massive **Charles Fort**, built in 1677. The Old Head of Kinsale has fine views and a castle. To its west lie the sandy strands of Garretstown.

◆◆◆
RING OF KERRY

This 100-mile (160km) route round the Iveragh Peninsula takes in some spectacular coastal scenery. Most organised tours – and there are many – start and end in Killarney. The circuit lasts around four hours by bus, but allow a full day if you are travelling independently and want to explore some detours. Even then, you will need another day to visit the Skelligs, and half a day for the centre of the peninsula. There are many prehistoric and early Christian remains; one of the easiest to find is **Staigue Fort**, on the south coast between Caherdaniel and Sneem, which dates from around 1000BC. The ancient past takes on a livelier form each August in the town of **Killorglin**, when it holds its three-day Puck Fair, presided over by a crowned goat. Other present-day settlements on the peninsula include the village of

Fishermen on the quay at Kinsale

Sneem, attractively clustered round two greens; **Waterville,** a popular resort with palm trees, a championship golf course and good fishing in the nearby large lake; and **Cahirciveen,** Daniel O'Connell's birthplace. Many of the peninsula's inhabitants are Gaelic speakers. Good beaches include Rossbeigh (looking across to Dingle): Ballinskelligs; and several near Caherdaniel. Inland there are many lakes, including beautiful Lough Carragh (part of the fine view from the top of Seefin). See also **Derrynane House, Kenmare** and the **Killarney Valley.**

◆◆
SKELLIG MICHAEL
off the Iveragh Peninsula
This is one of Ireland's most evocative early Christian sites. In about AD600, St Finan established a monastery on the small rocky island. The asceticism of the monks' lives is powerfully conveyed by the simple, small drystone buildings – windowless beehive huts and tiny oratories – which have survived attack by Vikings and the elements. The church is newer. Now, the three Skellig islands are uninhabited but for seabirds. Boats to Skellig Michael leave from Portmagee and Cahirciveen throughout the year, depending on weather and demand.

◆
TIMOLEAGUE
The grey ruined bulk of what was once Ireland's largest friary, founded in 1312, stands beside a muddy, wide estuary, frequented by flocks of waders. Overlooking the ruins are the small gardens of Timoleague Castle, with herbaceous borders, lawns and trees and a children's corner. The colourful village of Courtmacsherry nearby is a sea-angling centre.

Accommodation
Expensive:
Kenmare, Co Kerry: **Park Hotel Kenmare** 4-star (tel: (064) 41200) – superbly run, luxurious country hotel in Victorian mansion, set in extensive grounds overlooking the estuary; award-winning restaurant.
Killarney, Co Kerry: **Aghadoe Heights** 4-star (tel: (064) 31766) – medium-size modern hotel with fine lake and mountain views.

Medium:
Bantry, Co Cork. **Bantry House** (T&C)(tel: (027) 80047) – comfortable, attractive bedrooms in wings of superb stately home overlooking the Bay.
Dingle, Co Kerry: **Benner's,** Main Street (tel: (066) 51638) – restored former coaching inn.
Kinsale, Co Cork: **Scilly House** (T&C) (tel: (021) 772413) – small, stylishly decorated, with attractive gardens.

Cheap:
Ballinadee, near Bandon, Co Cork: **Glebe House** (T&C) (tel: (021) 778294) – thoughtfully run, Georgian house with period furniture; good food.
Blennerville, Tralee, Co Kerry: **Aharoe** (GH) (tel: (066) 23108) –

spotless, comfortable modern house.

Greenane, Kenmare, Co Kerry: **Templenoe House** (FH) (tel: (064) 41538) – 220-year-old house in village on the Ring of Kerry.

Kenmare, Co Kerry: **Glendarragh** (GH) (tel: (064) 41436) – comfortable modern house in beautiful setting off Castletownbere road; good food.

Restaurants
Expensive:
Kenmare, Co Kerry: **Park Hotel Kenmare** — see under **Accommodation**.

Medium:
Ballylickey, Co Cork: **Sea View House** — see under **Accommodation**.

Bantry, Co Cork: **O'Connor's Seafood** (tel: (027) 50221) – popular restaurant and bar specialising in Bantry Bay mussels.

Dingle, Co Kerry: **Doyle's Seafood Bar** (tel: (066) 51174) – relaxed, cosy restaurant, widely known for its excellent seafood and friendly owners; also B&B. Next door, less well known but just as good, and with an indoor garden, **Half-Door Restaurant** (tel: (066) 51600).

Killarney, Co Kerry: **Gaby's Seafood**, High Street (tel: (064) 32519) – established family-run bistro.

Killorglin, Co Kerry: **Nick's** (tel: (066) 61219) – relaxed, dark-beamed, with pianist; specialises in seafood.

Kinsale, Co Cork: **Jim Edwards**, Market Quay (tel: (021) 772541) – bar-restaurant.

Cheap:
Dingle, Co Kerry: **Eiri na Greine** — wholefood restaurant.

Skibbereen, Co Cork: **Kitchen Garden** — simple homemade snacks and lunches in restaurant at back of shop.

Timoleague, Co Cork: **Dillons** — brasserie-style pub serving good tea and coffee as well as snacks and meals.

Pointing the way at Timoleague

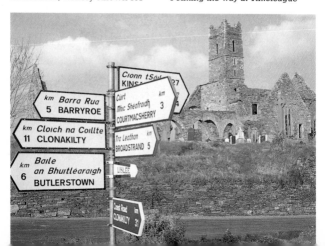

GALWAY AND THE WEST

GALWAY

The 'Capital of the West' has grown rapidly over the last few decades, spreading out from its attractively small-scale centre of old lanes and winding streets on the east bank of the Corrib river. Galway city has been the focus of efforts to revitalise the region, through the renaissance of Celtic culture and the Irish language, and by economic development. A university town, it also attracts many young travellers who add to its lively atmosphere. This, and its proximity to some of Ireland's finest scenery, are its main appeal to visitors. The city almost turns its back on the sea, but the suburb of Salthill is a popular resort. In medieval times, Galway prospered through trade, particularly with Spain; a present-day reminder of this is Spanish Arch, the only survivor of four arches built in 1594 to secure imports from Spain of wine and spirits. It now houses the tiny city museum. As in many other towns, the native Irish were evicted and created their own community, in this case on the west side of the Corrib river. Known as the Claddagh, the settlement developed its own customs and culture – the Claddagh ring, with its motif of crowned heart and clasped hands, originated here.

Old merchants' houses still exist around Shop Street, despite redevelopment.

WHAT TO SEE

◆
CHURCH OF ST NICHOLAS
Market Street
This large medieval church has a fine west doorway, gargoyles and other decorative medieval stonework including a canopied Lynch tomb. Many of the monuments bear the marks of damage inflicted by Cromwell's soldiery.

◆
LYNCH'S CASTLE
Shop Street
A rare survivor in Galway city of a 16th-century building, this merchant's house appropriately now houses a bank. Restored in the 19th century, it has a fine exterior with carved medallions and gargoyles and intricate window lintels.

◆
NORA BARNACLE'S HOUSE
Bowling Green
This one-up, one-down terraced house was the family home of the woman who later married James Joyce and inspired some of his characters, including Molly Bloom in *Ulysses*. Sparsely furnished as it would have been in her childhood, it also contains some Joyce memorabilia. Occasional literary talks are held here.

Accommodation
Expensive:
Great Southern 4-star, Eyre Square (tel: (091) 64041) – traditional city-centre 'grand

GALWAY AND
THE WEST

hotel', built in 1845, with all modern facilities including heated swimming pool.

Medium:
Ardilaun House 3-star, Taylor's Hill (tel: (091) 21433) – large converted and extended country house in private grounds, in easy reach of the leisure facilities of Salthill.

Cheap:
Inishmore House (T&C), 109 Father Griffin Road, Lower Salthill (tel: (091) 62639) – family house with garden.

Restaurants
There are plenty of good casual eating places around Shop Street, including pubs

part eating area; and Conlon and Sons, in Eglinton Street.

Expensive:
Drimcong House, near Moycullen, Co Galway (tel: (091) 85115) – a 20-minute drive out of the city, but well worth it for exceptional, imaginative cooking in an elegant setting. Choice of pricier full menu, excellent value set menu and cheaper children's and vegetarians' menus; dinner only.

Medium:
Eyre House, Forster Street (tel: (091) 62396) and, in the same building, **Park House** (tel: (091) 64924) – restaurant complex including a cellar grill, bar and lounge, serving above-average if unadventurous cooking.
Moran's Oyster Cottage, The Weir, Kilcolgan (tel: (091) 96113) – charming pub a short drive from town, reputed to serve the best oysters in Galway.
Rabbitts, Forster Street (tel: (091) 66490) – family run, with beer garden; mainly seafood and steaks.

Cheap:
Café Nora Crúb, 8 Quay Street (tel: (091) 68376) – comfortable, casual place for a drink, snack or full meal.
Millwheel Café, The Bridge Mills, O'Brien's Bridge – with pleasant waterside terrace.

Entertainment
To find out what's on, get the free *Galway Advertiser* (Thursdays) or *What's On in Galway* from the tourist office. Galway is the home of the national Irish-language theatre,

such as the Quays, in Quay Street, and Tigh Neachtain, in Cross Street, which often serves ethnic dishes.
Cheap and tasty ethnic food can also be eaten or taken away from the Toucan Café in Cross Street. Good places for fish include McDonagh's in Quay Street, part shop and

Capital of the west of Ireland, Galway is well worth exploring

Taibhdhearc na Gaillimhe, Middle Street (tel: (091) 62024), which stages bilingual productions in summer, often with traditional music. Traditional and other live music can be heard in many of the city's pubs, including the **King's Head** in Shop Street, **An Pucan** in Forster Street and **Tigh Neachtain** in Cross Street (where customers one night in September 1990 heard violinist Nigel Kennedy play an impromptu gig).

Shopping

Both Galway Crystal and Royal Tara China have factory shops on the outskirts of town. For tweed and Aran sweaters, try **O'Maille's** in Dominick Street. **The Bridge Mills**, by O'Brien's Bridge, is a converted 18th-century mill housing several craft studios as well as a wine bar and café, flower shop and secondhand bookshop. **Kenny's** bookshop in Quay Street has a wide selection of books about Ireland and by Irish authors; it backs on to an art gallery, also entered from Middle Street. **McDonagh's** in Quay Street has good smoked salmon, and **McCambridge's** delicatessen in Shop Street has a wide selection of farmhouse Irish cheeses. Locally made cheese and home baking, as well as fruit and vegetables, are sold in the Saturday open-air market, by St Nicholas Church.

and lived there intermittently through the 1920s. It then fell into decay, but has been restored once again to house an exhibition of Yeats's correspondence and work, including many first editions.

Accommodation
Expensive:
Ballyvaughan, Co Clare: **Gregans Castle** 3-star (tel: (065) 77005) – personally run country house hotel set in attractive gardens, on the edge of the Burren.
Newmarket-on-Fergus, Co Clare: **Dromoland Castle** 4-star (tel: (061) 71144) – fairytale castle charging princely prices, in extensive grounds with lake. Or stay with Lord and Lady Inchiquin (whose family seat the Castle was) in their rather smaller but also luxurious new home within the estate, **Thomond House** (tel: (061) 71304).

Medium:
Aglish, Co Tipperary: **Ballycormac House** (T&C) (tel: (067) 21129) – 300-year-old farmhouse three miles (5km) from Lough Derg, attractively furnished; excellent food.
Ballinderry, Co Tipperary: **Gurthalougha House** (tel: (067) 22080) – for real country-house atmosphere, hospitality and home cooking, in an early 19th-century house beside Lough Derg.
Birr, Co Offaly: **County Arms** 2-star, Railway Road (tel: (0509) 20791) – small family-run hotel in solid late-Georgian house in its own grounds; weekly traditional Irish night.
Lisdoonvarna, Co Clare:

Sheedy's Spa View 2-star (tel: (065) 74026) – family-run hotel with good restaurant.

Cheap:
Kilkee, Co Clare: **Halpin's** 1-star, Erin Street (tel: (065) 56032) – small family-run streetside hotel in seaside resort.
Horseleap, Co Westmeath: **Temple** (FH) (tel: (0506) 35118) – comfortable, charming 200-year-old house in peaceful setting.

Restaurants:
Expensive:
Ballyvaughan, Co Clare: **Claire's** (tel: (065) 29521) – accomplished cooking and friendly service in owner-run restaurant, part of craft shop and gallery; dinner and Sunday lunch only.
Bunratty, Co Clare: **MacCloskey's** (tel: (061) 364082) – intimate Irish-French restaurant in the whitewashed cellars of Bunratty House; dinner only.

Medium:
Bunratty, Co Clare: **Durty Nelly's** (tel: (061) 364861) – self-consciously characterful, rollicking pub specialising in Irish food; quieter meals in basement Oyster Bar or, for dinner, upstairs Loft Restaurant.

Cheap:
Ennis, Co Clare: **Dillinger's** – above-average pub food including ethnic dishes.
Kilronan Harbour, Inishmore, Aran Islands: **Youth Hostel Restaurant** (tel: (099) 61255) – daytime snacks and popular evening vegetarian meals.

NORTH AND WEST OF GALWAY

This area includes what some consider the most haunting scenery in Ireland. On parts of the coast, there is a real sense of being on the edge of the world, and inland there is a glorious combination of mountains and loughs. West of Galway city, the sea road leads through the boulder-strewn coastal lowlands of Irish-speaking Iar Connacht. Co Sligo to the north has many places associated with the poet W B Yeats. He spent childhood holidays in the area, and returned in later years.

◆
ACHILL ISLAND

Easier to reach than many of Ireland's western islands – a bridge joins it to the mainland – Achill is more built up as a result. The main attractions are the sandy beaches and splendid cliff scenery, for example at Keel village. In early summer, there is shark fishing (those who brave the chilly water need not fear, these are basking sharks). The quieter **Curraun Peninsula** is good for birdwatching.

◆◆
BALLINTUBBER ABBEY

near Ballintober
Founded in 1216, the abbey became a stopping place for pilgrims on the way to Croagh Patrick, visible in the distance. It has been in use for nearly eight centuries and is surrounded by a symbolic garden.

◆
BOYLE

An attractive riverside market town, Boyle has a well-preserved abbey on the outskirts. It was founded in 1235 and lies close to beautiful Lough Key, now part of a forest park. A couple of miles away, at Dromonone, is a dolmen called the Druid's Altar.

◆
CLARE ISLAND

The mountainous island was the home of Grace O'Malley, the 16th-century female pirate captain. You can still see remains of her castle stronghold, and of a 15th-century abbey, notable for its now much-faded frescos. Boats to Clare Island, **Caher Island** (which has remains of an early Christian settlement), and **Inishturk** (with a fine beach) leave from Roonah Quay, near the attractive village of Louisburg.

◆
CLIFDEN

The capital of Connemara, this appealing town was founded in the early 19th century in a beautiful setting by a sea inlet, with views of the Twelve Bens. It holds an Arts Festival in late September, and hosts the Connemara Pony Show in August, attracting buyers and breeders from all over the world. There are fine beaches near by, in Mannin Bay.

◆
CLONALIS HOUSE

near Castlerea
The Victorian mansion is the home of the O'Conors,

Achill Island's towering scenery

descendants of the last High Kings of Ireland. Its furnishings and displays include costumes and the harp of Ireland's last great bard, the blind Turlough O'Carolan.

◆
CONG

A good base for fishing in Lough Corrib, Cong also has a ruined abbey beside a tree-lined river, with fine doorways and other stonework, and a restored cloister. Nearby Ashford Castle, a Victorian successor to a Norman castle on this site, was built for the Guinness family and is now one of Ireland's most luxurious hotels. The grounds are open to the public.

◆
DRUMCLIFF

In his poem, 'Under Ben Bulben', W B Yeats set out clear instructions about his resting place in Drumcliff churchyard, down to the material – limestone – from which his headstone should be made; but he died in France in 1939, and it took until 1948 for his wishes to be carried out. Evidence of Drumcliff's past, as the site of a monastery founded in the 6th century, survives in part of a round tower and a carved 10th-century high cross. A road running east along the Drumcliff river (good for fishing) leads to Glencar Lough and a waterfall.

◆◆
LISSADELL HOUSE
near Drumcliff
One of the places with a Yeats connection, this is the family home of the Gore-Booths, built in the 1830s. Yeats became friends with two sisters: Eva, also a poet, and Constance, later Countess Markievicz, a fervent Irish nationalist. The two are commemorated, with the house, in one of Yeats's poems in which he remembers them as young girls 'in silk kimonos, both beautiful, one a gazelle'.

♦
ROSCOMMON

Nothing remains of the monastery founded in AD746 by St Coeman, but you can still see the ruins of a 13th-century Dominican friary. Look out for the tomb of Felim O'Conor, King of Connacht, his bones watched over by mail-clad knights rather than apostles. In the pleasant town centre is a fine courthouse, now a bank, opposite the large 18th-century county jail. A huge, ruined 13th-century castle stands on the outskirts of town.

♦♦
ROSS ERRILLY FRIARY
near Headford

This is Ireland's best-preserved Franciscan friary, built in the 14th century by a de Burgo though most dates from the late 15th century. There are several domestic buildings including a kitchen with water tank, as well as an arcaded cloister. Climb right to the top of the tower for a bird's eye view of it all.

♦♦
ROSSERK ABBEY

Standing beside the River Moy, Rosserk is an unusually well-preserved and atmospheric Franciscan friary, with many fine examples of stone carving. A short drive away, towards Killala, is another Franciscan ruin, **Moyne Abbey**, which has well-preserved cloisters. There is a round tower in **Killala** itself, a pleasant town rising up from a fishing harbour in a protected bay which offers good sea angling.

♦♦♦
SLIGO

Even if you are not one of the many on the Yeats pilgrimage, there is much to enjoy in and around this pleasant market town, many of whose shops still have traditional fronts. **Sligo Abbey**, founded in about 1250, was rebuilt in the 15th century but knocked down again two centuries later by Cromwell's army. It has some fine monuments and a well-preserved cloister. The **County Art Gallery**, above the library in Stephen Street, has a good collection of Irish paintings, including works by John Butler Yeats and Jack Yeats, respectively father and brother of W B. Next door, the **County Museum** includes a section devoted to the Yeats family. The **Yeats Building**, Hyde Bridge, has temporary art exhibitions and also hosts the annual Yeats International Summer School in August. **Doorly Park**, by the river, has views of Lough Gill and the mountains, and includes a race course. The **Hawk's Well Theatre** in Temple Street stages local and visiting productions, and in September Sligo holds a lively Arts Festival.

Not far from town is beautiful **Lough Gill**, one of whose islands is said to be the Innisfree of Yeats's poem. A circuit of the lough also takes in a number of interesting ruins including **Creevelea Abbey**, the last Franciscan foundation in Ireland, before the suppression of the monasteries, and the recently restored 17th-century fortified manor house, **Parke's Castle**, which now houses a visitors' centre.

To the west of Sligo town, the resort of **Strandhill** has a fine sandy beach, a golf course and Dolly's Cottage, a typical early 19th-century home. Strandhill is also the location of Sligo regional airport. On the summit of nearby Knocknarea Mountain is a prehistoric cairn, associated with Maeve (Mebh), Queen of Connaught in the 1st century AD, but probably built in about 3000BC. Another prehistoric site in this area is **Carrowmore**, the largest group of megalithic remains in Europe, though quarrying has damaged many of them.

Rosses Point, on the north side of Sligo Bay, is a resort with two good sandy beaches and a championship golf course.

◆◆
STROKESTOWN PARK HOUSE
Strokestown

Built in the 1730s for the Mahon family, this Palladian country house remained their home until 1979. It conveys vividly the picture of life in a 'big house' at the centre of a large estate. Rooms include a fine library with original Regency wallpaper and a remarkable Chippendale bookcase; a dining room whose two empty picture frames are reminders of the decline in family fortunes when heirlooms were sold; a delightful nursery; and a kitchen with a gallery, from which the lady of the house would issue instructions. Outbuildings are being

converted into a Famine Museum, due to open in spring 1992.

◆◆
WESTPORT HOUSE
Westport

This handsome Georgian mansion was completed in the late 18th century by James Wyatt. Its rooms are furnished with family portraits, Irish landscapes, old silver and antique furniture. There are also dungeons, gift and antique shops, and an art centre. The grounds have been developed into an amusement park.

Accommodation
Expensive:

Cong, Co Mayo: **Ashford Castle** (tel: (092) 46003) – Victorian castle in extensive grounds, including a golf course, overlooking Lough Corrib.

Medium:

Ballinafad, Recess, Co Galway: **Ballynahinch Castle** 3-star (tel: (095) 31006) – country house hotel in superb setting at foot of one of the Twelve Bens, beside a river.

Clifden, Co Galway: **Ardagh** 3-star (tel: (095) 21384) – small, family-run modern hotel

Sligo Town, County Sligo

GALWAY AND THE WEST

beside rocky bay.
Letterfrack, Co Galway:
Rosleague Manor (tel: (095)
41101) – Georgian house.
Riverstown, Co Sligo:
Coopershill House (T&C) (tel:
(071) 65108) – Georgian
mansion, highly regarded.
Roscommon, Co Roscommon:
Abbey 3-star, Galway Road
(tel: (0903) 26240) – Victorian
Gothic mansion.
Sligo, Co Sligo: **Ballincar
House** 3-star (tel: (071) 45361) –
extended country house in
pleasant gardens.

Cheap:
Boyle, Co Roscommon:
Rushfield (FH) (tel: (079) 62276)
– large, old-style farmhouse
near Lough Key Forest Park.
Clonbur, Co Galway: **Fairhill**
(GH) (tel: (092) 46176) – in quiet
village, good fishing nearby.
Moycullen, Co Galway:
Moycullen House (T&C) (tel:
(091) 85566) – large Arts and
Crafts house on hill above
Lough Corrib.
Mulrany, Co Mayo: **Rosturk
Woods** (GH) (tel: (098) 36264) –
overlooking the sea.
Roscommon, Co Roscommon:
Munsboro House (FH) (tel:
(0903) 26375) – Georgian house
with period furniture, in private
estate, two miles (3.2km) north.
Sligo, Co Sligo: **Hillside** (FH)
(tel: (071) 42808) – large
farmhouse on Glencar road;
log fires, farm produce.

Restaurants
Expensive:
Barna, Co Galway: **Ty Ar Mor**,
Sea Point (tel: (091) 92223) –
modern French cooking,
especially seafood.
Cong, Co Mayo: **Ashford

Castle, Connaught Room
Restaurant – see under
Accommodation.

Medium:
Clifden, Co Galway: **O'Grady's
Seafood**, Market Street (tel:
(095) 21450) – small, friendly,
good value, using fresh local
produce.
Letterfrack, Co Galway:
Rosleague Manor – see under
Accommodation.
Lough Arrow, Co Sligo:
Cromleach Lodge (tel: (071)
65155) – short but interesting
menu based on fresh local
produce; dinner only; B & B.
Westport, Co Mayo: **Quay
Cottage**, The Quay (tel: (098)
26412) – attractive little
waterside restaurant, both
decor and food inspired by
fish and shellfish.

Cheap:
Keel, Achill Island, Co Mayo:
Chalet Seafood (tel: (098)
43157) – simple dishes based
on fresh seafood, including
home-smoked salmon.
Knocknahur, Co Sligo: **Coolera
House** (tel: (071) 68204) –
family-run restaurant with good
home cooking.
Mulrany, Co Mayo: **Old Post
Office Café** (tel: (098) 36247) –
teashop, usually open till early
evening.
Roscommon, Co Roscommon:
Westdeli – roadside daytime
café serving above-average
snacks and simple meals.
Sligo, Co Sligo: **Truffles**, The
Mall (tel: (071) 44226) –
especially good for pizzas.
Westport, Co Mayo:
Continental Café (tel: (098)
26679) – simple homemade
wholefood.

BELFAST AND THE NORTH

BELFAST

Northern Ireland's capital and the second largest city in the whole of Ireland has achieved worldwide fame for the worst of reasons: the sectarian conflicts of recent years. Yet a visitor to Belfast is in far less danger than in many large cities: excluding those conflicts, levels of personal violence, in the form of muggings and the like, are remarkably low. Most of the city centre is safe at all times; the areas where any trouble would be likely to flare up are the outlying residential suburbs, particularly of west and north Belfast. The crime that residents and visitors have to beware most is joyriding – stealing cars and driving them in crazy fashion. The answer is to park in secured parking lots, or to take cabs.

City Hall – Belfast's civic pride

Belfast's recent troubled history tends to obscure its flourishing past. In 1842 it was described by the author William Thackeray as 'as neat, prosperous, and handsome a city as need be seen . . . It looks hearty, thriving and prosperous, as if it had money in its pockets and roast beef for dinner.' Largely born out of the 18th- and 19th-century industrial revolution, it expanded rapidly with the introduction of the textile industry. It was, and still is, an important port, in a fine sheltered position on the banks of the Lagan river at its entry into Belfast Lough – the city's name comes from the Irish, *beal feirste*, meaning 'mouth of the sandy ford'. Shipbuilding brought more work and prosperity, though this and other manufacturing industries have declined in recent times. Today the city is undergoing extensive redevelopment, but the centre retains its essentially Victorian character,

with imposing public buildings and churches and, on the river side, red-brick warehouses and factories, many empty or converted to new uses.

WHAT TO SEE IN THE CITY CENTRE

◆◆◆
CITY HALL
Donegall Square
This is impossible to miss, which must be just what the confident Victorian city fathers intended. Built in 1898–1906 of Portland limestone, it features a copper-covered dome and lantern. The interior, lavishly decorated with fine marbles, is open for tours on Wednesday mornings.

◆◆◆
CROWN LIQUOR SALOON
Great Victoria Street
A popular rendezvous, this fine example of an ornate, gaslit Victorian pub, with snug little wood-panelled compartments, was restored to its full glory by the National Trust.

◆◆
GRAND OPERA HOUSE
Great Victoria Street
The matchless theatre architect Frank Matcham designed this traditional Victorian theatre. Well restored, it combines Matcham's delightful Indian Raj auditorium – look out for the elephants' heads – with pleasant, spacious bars.

◆◆
LINEN HALL LIBRARY
Donegall Square North

Charming and old-fashioned, the library has plenty of comfortable seats tucked away among wooden shelves of books which include many works on Ireland, and on the linen trade in particular. It also stocks daily newspapers and magazines, and there is a small tearoom. The library was founded in 1788, and takes its name from its original home, the old White Linen Hall.

Expensive:
Culloden 4-star, 142 Bangor
Road, Holywood (tel: (023 17)
5223) – Northern Ireland's top
hotel, a former bishop's palace
with extensions, five miles
(8km) northeast of the centre;
new leisure complex.
Europa, Great Victoria Street
(tel: (0252) 327000) – large,
modern and central.

Medium:
Dukes 65–7 University Street,
Belfast BT7 1HB (tel: (0232)
236666) – small new hotel on
corner of Botanic Avenue.
Plaza, 15 Brunswick Street,
Belfast BT2 7GE (tel: (0232)
333555) – central, smart
business and tourist hotel.
Stormont 3-star, 587 Upper
Newtownards Road (tel: (0232)
658621) – modern hotel
overlooking grounds of Stormont
Castle, four miles (6km) east of
the centre.
Wellington Park, 21 Malone
Road (tel: (0232) 381111) –
medium-sized hotel with spacious
bedrooms, busy bars used by
local architects and lawyers.

Cheap:
Ash-Rowan (GH), 12 Windsor
Avenue (tel: (0232) 661758) –
Victorian house in southern
suburb, upmarket in style,
above-average prices.
Camera (GH), 44 Wellington
Park (tel: (0232) 660026) –
comfortable Victorian house
near Queen's University.

Restaurants
Many of Belfast's eating places
are to be found in two districts,
the 'Golden Mile' – Great
Victoria Street, leading to
Shaftesbury Square – and the

Palm House, Botanic Gardens

university area. You can find
just about every cuisine in
more or less authentic form,
with the almost total exception
of Northern Irish cooking
above the level of an Ulster
fry. Few restaurants are open
on Sundays.

Expensive:
Roscoff, Lesley House,
Shaftesbury Square (tel: (0232)
331532) – Michelin 1-star
establishment, Roux-trained
chef. This is Northern Ireland's
leading restaurant.
Schooner, 30 High Street,
Holywood (tel: (0232) 428880) –
original, varied menu; open for
Sunday lunch.

Medium:
La Belle Epoque, 103 Great
Victoria Street (tel: (0232)
323244) – good bistro,
attractively designed;
evenings only.
Culloden – see under
Accommodation; open on
Sundays.
Manor House, 47 Donegall
Pass (tel: (0232) 238755) –
Cantonese Chinese food.

Metropolitan, 78 Botanic Avenue (tel: (0232) 332626) – pleasant bistro with French owner but wide-ranging menu, from pasta to pork pies.

Nick's Warehouse, Hill Street (tel: (0232) 439690) – enthusiastically run wine bar and upstairs restaurant with good food and well-priced wine, closed at weekends.

Strand, 12 Stranmillis Road (tel: (0232) 682266) – good-value meals in very popular wine bar-cum-restaurant.

Cheap:

Crown Liquor Saloon, 46 Great Victoria Street (tel: (0232) 249476) – oysters in season, and some Irish dishes.

Front Page, 106 Donegall Street (tel: (0232) 324924) – specialising in seafood; live traditional music.

Entertainment

Two monthly news-sheets, *Artslink* and *What's On*, give advance details of the main attractions; and the *Belfast Telegraph* carries listings, particularly the Friday edition, as do the *News Letter* and *Irish Press*. Belfast has three main theatres and several music venues, from concert-halls to pubs with traditional and other live music.

Shopping

The district immediately north of City Hall, much of it pedestrianised, is the main shopping area, and includes the large new Castle Court complex. Most shops stay open late on Thursdays. Stockists of Irish linen include **Halls**, in the attractive Queen's Arcade; the department store **Anderson and McAuley**, in Donegall Place; and the **Irish Linen Store**, the Fountain Centre, College Street. Gift shops and department stores stock a range of other Northern Ireland products including handmade Tyrone crystal and Belleek china. For good examples of modern design from Ireland and abroad, try **Equinox**, in Howard Street.

Room to relax in a city bar

NORTH AND WEST OF BELFAST

WHAT TO SEE

◆
BALLYCASTLE

This market town retains its attractive, largely Georgian centre. The delightful church on one side of the Diamond houses several monuments to the Boyd family, who developed the town in the 18th century. The harbour area is more obviously geared to the demands of the summer tourist trade.

Ballycastle's Ould Lammas Fair, at the end of August, is the oldest such event in Ireland. **Bonamargy Friary**, a short way out of town, is the burial place of Sorley Boy MacDonnell, 16th-century ancestor of the earls of Antrim. **Rathlin Island** can be visited by boat from Ballycastle Harbour: the island is where the Scottish hero Robert the Bruce is said to have been inspired by the perseverance of a spider.

◆
BUSHMILLS

On the bank of the River Bush is a small, prosperous town whose name is spoken far and wide – usually in a bar or pub, for Bushmills is the name and the home of an Irish whiskey. The distillery is open for guided tours on weekdays; in the high season, phone first to reserve a place (tel: (02657) 31521). A couple of miles west of town is the ruin of **Dunluce Castle**, built in about 1300 for Richard de Burgh.

Making music in Ballycastle

◆◆
CARRICKFERGUS

This historic town is still dominated visually if not socially by the splendid harbourside castle built in 1180 by the Norman lord, John de Courcy. Parts of the church of St Nicholas are Norman, though much of the present structure dates from restoration work in 1614. Short stretches of the medieval town wall survive, including the restored Irish Gate near the church. On the outskirts of town, at Boneybefore, is the **Andrew Jackson Centre**, a little museum about the US president's family, who emigrated from their home near by in 1765.

◆◆
CASTLE COOLE
near Enniskillen
Set in attractive parkland and overlooking a lake, this very grand neo-classical mansion of the 1790s was designed by James Wyatt. Now owned by the National Trust, its impeccably restored and decorated interior features several superb plasterwork ceilings and fine antique furniture.
The house closes during the winter but the grounds are open all year.

◆
DONEGAL
A small town set on the wooded shores of the River Eske, Donegal began as a Viking settlement, and grew as the main stronghold of the O'Donnells. After the defeat of the Irish leaders in 1607, it was granted to Sir Basil Brooke, who laid out the town, including its large central square, the Diamond. He also converted the O'Donnell castle into his home, adding a manor house and decorative features such as a richly carved chimney piece. The town's other ancient building is a ruined waterside friary. Tweed-weaving demonstrations are given in Magee's, on the Diamond; and just south of town there is a purpose-built 'craft village' of workshops, open daily except Sundays.

◆◆
FANAD PENINSULA
A circuit of this peninsula, which lies between Lough Swilly and Mulroy Bay, takes in some superb scenery and several attractive villages. These include **Rathmullan**, the port which in 1607 witnessed the 'Flight of the Earls' when the defeated Irish nobles, led by the heads of the O'Neill and O'Donnell families, quit Ireland. A small interpretative centre, near the pier, provides more information on this seminal event. **Ramelton** (spelt Rathmelton on some maps) was the birthplace of Francis Makemie, founder of the Presbyterian Church in the US. It has some fine old harbour warehouses and good fishing.

◆◆◆
FLORENCE COURT
south of Enniskillen, off A32
This fine mid-18th-century mansion, now owned by the National Trust, is set in grounds with views of the surrounding mountains. Its elegant interior includes some exuberant plasterwork.

◆◆◆
GIANT'S CAUSEWAY
near Bushmills
The curious rock shapes along this stretch of coast have intrigued generations of visitors. As the visitors' centre explains, the basalt columns were created by volcanic eruption, some 55 million years ago. Fanciful names have been given to many of the formations, of which the hexagonal-columned Causeway is only one. A minibus runs between the visitors' centre and the Causeway, but the best way to enjoy the cliff and sea views is by one of the circular walks,

shown and described in a pamphlet available from the National Trust's shop within the centre.

To the east of the Causeway is Port-na-Spaniagh Bay, where the Armada ship the *Girona* was smashed on the rocks. Items recovered from the wreck are on display in Belfast's Ulster Museum. Also along this stretch of coast, a number of spectacular caves can be reached by boat.

♦♦
GLEBE HOUSE AND GALLERY
near Church Hill
Once the home of artist Derek Hill, who gave it to the state, this Regency house on the shores of Lough Gartan is furnished and decorated in a delightfully idiosyncratic mix of styles. Hill's gift included his collection of mainly 20th-century art, housed in the adjoining Glebe Gallery, which includes works by Picasso, Bonnard, Sutherland and others as well as Donegal folk art.

The Gartan Lough area is where Ireland's great saint, Columba, was born in AD521; his life and times are recounted at the nearby **Colmcille Heritage Centre**.

♦
GLENCOLUMBKILLE FOLK VILLAGE
Beside Glen Bay, in an area dotted with prehistoric remains and ruined churches, are three reconstructed cottages representing rural homes of the 1920s, 1820s and 1720s, together with an old school house and replicas of other village structures such as a lime kiln. There is also a craft shop and a tearoom. Each year on St Columba's day, 9 June, a pilgrimage takes in many of the valley's ancient sites.

The unique Giant's Causeway

Glenarm on the coast of Antrim

♦♦
GLENVEAGH NATIONAL PARK
near Church Hill
A 25,000-acre (10,000-hectare) park in a superb setting of mountains and loughs, it contains a dramatically sited castle (1870) set in gardens. Both are open to visitors and reached by free minibus from the visitors' centre (last bus 90 minutes before the park closes). The park has a nature trail, and there are guided walks in July and August.

♦♦♦
GLENS OF ANTRIM
This name is given to the area roughly east of an imaginary line between Ballycastle and Ballymena, encompassing some of Ireland's most romantically dramatic scenery. There are traditionally nine glens – careful map readers

may spot a few more – of which the best known is Glenariff, now part of a forest park, with some beautiful waterfalls. Attractive villages and towns in the area include **Glenarm**, on the southern shore of Carnlough Bay, with a neat main street of Georgian and Victorian houses, and a turreted castle. Nearby Carnlough has a sandy beach. The town of **Glenariff**, also called Waterfoot, holds a festival of Irish music and dancing each July. The National Trust protects both the village and beach of **Cushendun**, with its whitewashed, slate-hung cottages designed by the 20th-century architect Clough Williams-Ellis, best known for his creation of Portmeirion, in North Wales.

♦♦
INISHOWEN PENINSULA
Ireland's northernmost point, Malin Head, is one of the viewpoints included in the 'Inis Eoghain 100' – a signposted motoring circuit of this mountainous peninsula. Places of interest on the west side include **Fahan**, with a good beach and, in the churchyard, an 8th-century cross-slab; the **Vintage Car Museum** at Buncrana; **Tullyarvan Mill** just north of Buncrana; and the **Fort Dunree Military Museum** at Dunree, on the shore of Lough Swilly. On the outskirts of **Carndonagh** is an 8th-century cross flanked by two carved stones; and, on a hill just west of the Derry border, there is a particularly fine restored ringfort, the **Grianán of Aileach**.

◆
LONDONDERRY
This historic city and port has suffered many assaults over the centuries, not least during this century. Its very name – Londonderry or Derry – is a subject for dispute. One media wit's answer is to refer to it as Stroke City (alluding to the unspoken oblique between the two versions of the name). Despite its notoriety, the city has attractions for the visitor. The 17th-century **City Walls** that withstood 105 days of siege by James II's army in 1688–9 have remained intact, and there are fine views from the promenade along the parapet.

◆
LOUGH ERNE
Scattered through both the Lower and Upper parts of the lough are over 150 islands, some carrying the ruins of early Christian or pagan settlements. **Boa Island**, the largest on Lower Lough Erne and joined to the mainland by bridges, has two pagan double-sided idols. **Devenish Island** has a fine round tower and ruined Augustinian abbey, notable for their carved decorations (ferry from Trory, Easter to September, daily except Mondays; or waterbus from Enniskillen, as part of a two-hour cruise). On **White Island**, a line of eight carved stone figures, unearthed over the period 1840–1958, now stare out inscrutably from beside a medieval church. It can be reached by ferry in summer from the marina in **Castle Archdale** country park.

Two of Upper Lough Erne's most interesting islands, **Cleenish** and **Inishkeen**, can be reached by foot. A number of companies rent out cabin cruisers.

◆◆
MARBLE ARCH CAVES
near Florence Court
Formed by rivers flowing underground (one of which emerges into the delightful glen below), these caves with their rock formations are explored partly by boat and partly on foot on a 90-minute tour. Phone first to reserve a place (tel: (0365) 82777).

◆
MUSSENDEN TEMPLE
The Temple of Vesta in Rome inspired this classical temple, just west of the little resort of Castlerock, on cliffs overlooking an attractive stretch of coast. Now in the care of the National Trust, it was built in the 1780s for the Bishop of Derry and Earl of Bristol, Frederick Hervey, whose ecumenical campaigns included organising races between clergy of all denominations on nearby Magilligan Strand.

◆◆
SHANE'S CASTLE
near Antrim
The family seat of the Clandeboye O'Neills, the castle itself is a substantial ruin, except for a conservatory, designed by John Nash, which shelters camellias. The large estate, overlooking Lough Neagh, can be explored on foot and, on certain days, by

narrow-gauge steam railway. Other attractions include herds of deer and rare breeds of cattle, a small fairground and a nature reserve. Special events in summer include steam, vintage car and traction engine rallies.

◆◆
SPRINGHILL
near Moneymore
A rare survivor from the late 17th century, part of this very attractive whitewashed house has its origins back in the Plantation period in Ireland. It remained the home of the Conyngham family for three centuries, and is still fitted out with their furniture, portraits and other personal possessions. Large outbuildings contain a costume collection. The attractive grounds include walled gardens and woods.

◆◆◆
ULSTER–AMERICAN FOLK PARK
near Omagh, off A5
Thomas Mellon left Ulster for

Ulster – American Folk Park

the New World in 1818, at the age of five, and his descendants' wealth has helped to establish this folk park around their ancestral home. A number of representative old buildings have been rebuilt on the wooded site to illustrate traditional Irish village life; several are staffed by costumed guides or craftworkers, such as a weaver in the weaver's cottage. A street of 19th-century shopfronts leads to a building containing a full-size replica of the kind of ship that carried the emigrants across the Atlantic, on a voyage that might take 35 days or, as in the Mellons' case, twice that time, thanks to bad winds. Thence the route leads to a reconstructed Western Pennsylvanian settlement, with log cabin, log farmhouse and other buildings.

◆
ULSTER HISTORY PARK
near Omagh, off B48
Close to the Gortin Glen Forest Park, this new theme park

presents the history of Ireland's inhabitants from around 7000BC to the mid-17th century, through a series of replicated buildings and monuments.

◆
WELLBROOK BEETLING MILL
near Cookstown
An 18th-century water-powered mill used in the final stages of linen manufacture has been restored to working order by the National Trust. It makes a pleasant place for riverside walks. **Beaghmore**, a short drive west, is an extraordinary prehistoric site with no fewer than seven stone circles.

Accommodation
Expensive:
Dunadry, Co Antrim: **Dunadry Inn** (tel: (084 94) 32474) – attractive whitewashed hotel in own grounds, handy for international airport; good restaurant.
Fivemiletown, Co Tyrone: **Blessingbourne** (T&C) (tel: (036 55) 21221) – Victorian Gothic lakeside mansion in large estate, antiques and curios (unsuitable for children).

Medium:
Coleraine, Co Londonderry: **Blackheath House** (T&C), Blackhill (tel: (0265) 868433) – comfortable old rectory in landscaped gardens, with indoor pool; good restaurant.
Killybegs, Co Donegal: **Bruckless House** (FH) (tel: (073) 37071) – Georgian, in seaside setting between Donegal and Killibegs; log fires, homegrown and local food.

Larne, Co Antrim: **Magheramorne House** (tel: (0574) 79444) – Victorian mansion in woodland setting.
Rathmullan, Co Donegal: **Rathmullan House** (tel: (074) 58188) – welcoming country house hotel with good restaurant, in grounds overlooking Lough Swilly.
Rossnowlagh, Co Donegal: **Sand House** 3-star (tel: (072) 51777) – comfortable hotel with traditional ambience, lovely setting beside Donegal Bay.

Cheap:
Aghadowey, Co Londonderry: **Greenhill House** (T&C) (tel: (0265) 868241) – attractively renovated late Georgian farmhouse in River Bann valley, home cooking.
Ballycastle, Co Antrim: **Antrim Arms** (tel: (026 57) 62284) – friendly streetside old inn.
Belcoo, Co Fermanagh: **Corralea Forest Lodge** (T&C) (tel: (036 586) 325) – modern, with fine lough views, set in wooded nature reserve.
Florence Court, Co Fermanagh: **Tullyhona House** (FH) (tel: (036 582) 452) – comfortable modern house in attractive countryside; good cooking.
Giant's Causeway, Co Antrim: **Hillcrest House** (F&C) (tel: (026 57) 31577) – modern and comfortable, overlooking sea.
Portballintrae, Co Antrim: **White Gables** (GH) (tel: (026 57) 31611) – modern family house on coast road with superb views.
Portrush, Co Antrim: **Ballymagarry** (GH), Looke Road (tel: (0265) 823737) – well run, friendly and comfortable.

Also **Maddybenny Farm** (FH),
Loguestown Road (tel: (0265)
823394) – modern, friendly and
comfortable, award-winning
breakfasts.

Restaurants
Expensive:
Dunadry, Co Antrim: **Dunadry
Inn** – see under
Accommodation.

Medium:
Bellanaleck, Co Fermanagh:
The Sheelin (tel: (036 582) 232)
– thatched cottage bakery
which also serves daytime
snacks and teas in high
summer; Saturday dinner.
Bundoran, Co Donegal:
Landhaus (tel: (072) 41915) –
relaxed hospitality and tasty
German food; dinner only.
Fahan, Co Donegal: **Restaurant
St John's** (tel: (077) 60289) –
simple, traditional-style food
and well-priced wine.
Newtownabbey, Co Antrim:
Sleepy Hollow (tel: (0232)
342042) – in art gallery, out of
the ordinary; dinner only.

Cheap:
Augher, Co Tyrone:
Rosamund's Coffee Shop (tel:
(066 25) 48601) – lunches and
daytime snacks.
Enniskillen, Co Fermanagh:
Blake's of the Hollow (tel:
(0365) 22143) – good
sandwiches in Victorian pub.
Florence Court, Co
Fermanagh: **Florence Court
House** (tel: (036 582) 249) –
simple home cooking, lunches
and teas.
Londonderry, Co Londonderry:
Linenhall Bar (tel: (0504)
371665) – good pub food;
lunchtime only.

EAST AND SOUTH OF BELFAST

For variety and charm, this
area is hard to beat. Its
scenery ranges from the open,
wild uplands of the Mourne
Mountains to the sheltered
little bays of Strangford Lough.
There is a strong army
presence in South Armagh,
and patrols and checkpoints
are a common sight; if you
don't let this put you off, you
will find the countryside
unspoilt and the people
friendly.

WHAT TO SEE

◆
ANNALONG
The attractive little harbour,
against a backdrop of the
Mournes, is overlooked by a
restored 19th-century corn mill
with a display on water power.
There is a visitors' shop and
café nearby.

◆◆
ARDRESS HOUSE
near Portadown
A 17th-century farmhouse
extended and given
fashionably classical façades
in the 1770s, this National Trust
property contains some superb
18th-century plasterwork as
well as fine furniture and
paintings. The cobbled
farmyard houses both
equipment and animals; and
there are woodland walks, a
garden and a children's
playground.

◆◆◆
ARDS PENINSULA
This narrow, low-lying curve of
land protecting Strangford

Lough from the Irish Sea has attracted settlers for centuries. Its sandy beaches, pretty scenery and varied recreational facilities now bring many summer visitors, and there are lots of camping and caravan sites and guesthouses. Pleasant towns and villages include **Bangor**, its Edwardian seafront now overlooking a large modern marina; earlier buildings include the tower of the Abbey Church, near the rail station. A Heritage Centre has displays of local archaeological finds. South of Bangor is the market town of **Newtownards**, with a handsome 18th-century town hall, now an arts centre, and a 17th-century market cross. The dominant landmark in this area is a hilltop tower standing within **Scrabo Country Park**; built as a memorial to the 3rd Marquis of Londonderry, it now houses an exhibition. Climb the 122 steps up to be rewarded by splendid views over Strangford Lough. Just east, on the Millisle road, is ruined **Movilla Abbey**, which incorporates a number of 13th-century coffin lids.

Donaghadee has a large harbour with a lighthouse, and a pub – Grace Neill's in High Street – which first opened for business in 1611. To its south, near Millisle, is **Ballycopeland Windmill**, built in the late 18th century, with a visitors' centre in the miller's house. On the lough side, not far from Mount Stewart (see separate entry), **Grey Abbey** is the substantial ruin of a 12th-century Cistercian friary. At the southern end of the Ards, in Portaferry, the **Northern Ireland Aquarium** shows the rich variety of Strangford Lough's marine life. Adjacent outdoor attractions include a wildfowl pond and children's playground. From Portaferry harbour, there is a frequent, year-round car and passenger ferry service across the lough to Strangford village.

◆◆◆
THE ARGORY
near Moy

Set in a wooded estate beside the Blackwater river, this solid neo-classical 1820s mansion has a delightful interior, hardly altered since the beginning of this century. The contents are a mix of fine antique furniture, family possessions and curios such as an 1824 barrel organ. Some of the rooms are still lit by a 1906 acetylene gas plant.

Grey Abbey's ruined glory

The grand stable yard incorporates a coach house, harness room, laundry and the gas plant.

◆◆◆
ARMAGH

Capital of the ancient kingdom of Ulster, Armagh was appointed Ireland's ecclesiastical centre by St Patrick in AD447. The latest of many churches on the site of St Patrick's own is the **Protestant cathedral**; though mainly 19th-century, it contains several fine 18th-century monuments, and a slab marks the burial place of Brian Ború, High King of Ireland. The hilltop Gothic-style **Roman Catholic cathedral** was finished in 1873; with its twin spires, it looks particularly handsome from the Moy road. Armagh's most attractive buildings are Georgian; they include the townhouses lining the wide, tree-flanked green of the **Mall**, one of which houses the excellent **County Museum**. At one end of the Mall stands the fine classical **courthouse**. Other fine buildings include the **archbishop's palace**, built in the 1770s, beside which stands a chapel in the style of an Ionic temple; and, in the palace grounds, the ruins of a 13th-century **Franciscan friary**. Armagh's delightful **observatory** also dates from the 1770s, but the very latest high-tech equipment is used for interactive displays and presentations in the modern **Planetarium**. Star shows are usually on Saturdays, but are daily in July and August –

reservations advisable, tel: (0861) 523689. Armagh holds an arts festival in October.

West of the city, **Navan Fort** is a large grass-covered mound enclosed by a ditch and bank. It was the site of the main residence of Ulster's royal rulers from around 700BC to AD332. Many legends are associated with Eamhain Mhacha, as it was called, including one that it gave Armagh its name.

◆
BESSBROOK

This pleasingly neat model town, built in the 19th century by a Quaker linen manufacturer, is approached through checkpoints because of the proximity of a large army barracks. From it, a road leads south to **Derrymore House**, a late 18th-century rustic fantasy.

◆◆◆
CASTLE WARD
near Strangford

A monument to marital incompatibility, this unique 18th-century house combines two distinct and clashing architectural styles: neo-classical and neo-Gothic. The former was the preference of the husband, Bernard Ward, later 1st Lord Bangor; the latter the taste of his wife, Anne. The difference between the east and west façades is strange enough; but the interior is both disconcerting and entrancing, as you pass from pure, cool, symmetrical elegance into rich, even fantastical decoration, culminating in the excessively

PEACE AND QUIET

Wildlife and Countryside in Ireland
by Paul Sterry

Introduction

Large parts of Ireland seem to have been genuinely untouched by time. Much of the scenery remained unchanged for centuries, and even now the wildlife often appears to co-exist in harmony with man and his activities. Visit any quiet rural area – rough meadow, bog, river, coast or woodland – and you will find a wealth of plants and animals. Almost anywhere is likely to prove exciting for those who love nature and wild places, but the following habitats and places, described from south to north of Ireland, may be of particular interest.

Turloughs

Turloughs are shallow lakes which are fed by ground water; the water level in them often fluctuates greatly and they may dry out altogether in the summer months. They often have an excellent variety of wild flowers, and they are usually good for birds, especially during the winter months. Sadly, these interesting habitats are fast declining in Ireland, victims of changes in land use.

One of the best remaining turloughs is at Rahasane, near Craughwell in Galway. During the winter months, Greenland white-fronted geese, wigeon, shovelers, lapwings and golden plovers can all be numerous around the grassy margins of the lake. Both Bewick's and whooper swans also visit Rahasane in winter, and the site gives a good opportunity to compare these two very similar birds. Although birds are generally numerous, the exact species present and the numbers vary markedly according to the prevailing water level.

Birds of the Coast

Ireland has an extremely varied coastline and one which, in the main, is comparatively unspoilt and undisturbed. The scenery varies from some of the most impressive and towering sea cliffs in Europe to tranquil estuaries, sandy beaches, dunes and shingle beaches. The birdlife benefits from this variety and, whatever the time of year, there is always something to see on the coast. Sea cliffs and offshore islands, especially on the west coast, have some of the best seabird colonies in Europe. Puffins, guillemots, black guillemots, razorbills, kittiwakes, gannets and fulmars are all locally common. They can usually be seen both on the cliffs and flying out to sea, sometimes in the company of nocturnal visitors to the colonies: Manx shearwaters and storm petrels. Seabird colonies are generally deserted after the end of August but the birds can still be seen offshore. Among the best cliff sites are Howth Head, just north of Dublin, Bray Head to the south, Helvick Head, just south of Dungarvan in Waterford and Horn Head near Dunfanaghy in Donegal. The Cliffs of Moher and much of the Mayo coast are also good and are covered later in this section. Estuaries and mudflats are wonderful places for waders and wildfowl, especially outside the breeding season. Try North Bull Island in Dublin Bay for superb views.

Blanket Bogs

Blanket bogs are among the most outstanding botanical features of Ireland: a thick layer of underlying peat acts like a sponge and supports a rich bog flora; sometimes mosses form a blanketing layer across open water. Here and there, islands of raised ground support plant species that prefer drier soils and add to the variety of the habitat. Unfortunately, drainage and peat extraction are now threatening these fragile and vulnerable habitats.

One of the best blanket bogs left is at Errisbeg, near Roundstone, in Co Galway. It is largely inaccessible due to the nature of the terrain, but visitors should still be able to see a wide range of bog plants as well as several species of heathers. The presence of Mediterranean heath is an indication of the so-called 'Lusitanian' influence on the wildlife of southwest Ireland, where flowers more at home in Portugal and Spain occur well outside their normal geographical range.

Hay Meadows

To the rural community, hay was, and still is, important as a fodder crop, cut in the summer and fed to livestock in winter and early spring. Although modern methods of production and harvesting are becoming increasingly prevalent, traditional hand-cutting still persists, especially in the west of Ireland. An attractive consequence of this method is that a dazzling array of colourful flowers is ensured every year in spring because the plants have time to set seed.

Although grasses comprise a major part of the hay crop, a lack of herbicides ensures that more colourful flowers can

Corncrakes

More than any other species, the corncrake is a bird whose fate is linked inextricably with the decline in hay meadows and changes in agricultural practices. Once, the grating 'crek-crek' call was a familiar sound across much of the British Isles. However, with agricultural mechanisation and the change in land use to cereal production, Ireland is now one of its last strongholds. Corncrakes, which you are far more likely to hear than to see, nest in the meadows and feed on insects and other invertebrates. The application of pesticides has an obvious consequence for the birds as does mechanical harvesting, especially when the field is harvested for silage, earlier in the year than would be the case for hay. Because they are ground-nesters, corncrakes often have their nests or broods destroyed by this practice.

also grow. Look for yellow heads of hay rattle, as well as dandelions, bedstraws, campions and spotted orchids. The grasses should not be dismissed as drab, however – when in flower they too can be surprisingly rich in colour of a subtle sort.

Clear Island
Also known as Cape Clear, the island lies in the far southwest of Ireland in Co Cork. It has a reputation for being one of the best sites in the country for observing bird migration and is especially good for unusual species. Although comparatively difficult to visit – it is reached by boat from the little village of Baltimore and only limited accommodation is available – the effort is usually rewarded, especially in spring and autumn. To reach Baltimore, follow the coastal N71 to Skibbereen and then head south to the end of the road.

The best time to watch the

Corncrake in a hay meadow

birds for which the sea around Clear Island are famous is when strong gales are blowing, but don't be put off, this can be a very exciting pastime! Thousands of gannets, kittiwakes, puffins, guillemots, terns and storm petrels stream by close to shore and, on good days, more unusual species can be found. Great skuas are regular in autumn and Manx shearwaters are often accompanied by sooty shearwaters, great shearwaters and Cory's shearwaters. One of the most unusual sightings from Clear Island was of a black-browed albatross, a bird which should normally be found in the seas of the southern hemisphere. The island itself has a good range of breeding birds, especially choughs, handsome members of the crow family with glossy black plumage and bright red beaks.

The Kerry Coast
Valentia Island boasts some of the most attractive coastal scenery in the country. To reach it, follow the coastal N70 to Cahirciveen and turn off west to the island. Seabirds and sometimes even whales and dolphins can be seen offshore, and the island attracts migrant birds, especially in autumn. Puffin Island – a seabird island – can be reached from Valentia by boat: it has a large colony of Manx shearwaters, a species not easy to see by day, as well as fulmars, kittiwakes, razorbills, shags and, naturally, puffins. Inland from the coast, the

PEACE AND QUIET

Valentia Island, County Kerry

Glengarrif Woods are interesting for their 'Lusitanian' (Portugese) influence. The presence of strawberry trees alongside rowan and birch trees is an indication of the unusual mixture of species to be found in southwest Ireland. The strawberry tree is a common species around the Mediterranean and in Portugal. The flowers are creamy white; the fruits are red and resemble a strawberry.

Akeragh Lough

This slightly brackish lough lies on the Kerry coast just south of Ballyheighe Bay. Protected from the force of the Atlantic by sand dunes, the waters are a haven for wintering wildfowl and waders. However, Akeragh Lough is probably more renowned for the variety and numbers of rare American waders that it attracts in autumn.

Normally, these birds migrate south from their breeding grounds in North America to the warmer climates of Central and South America. But each year, a few get blown off course and end up crossing the Atlantic, often making their first landfall on the Irish coast. Akeragh Lough's proximity to the coast, and the lack of similar sites near by, make it one of the most attractive spots for these tired migrants. Some spend several days feeding, preening and resting here before continuing their journey south.

Species seen here recently have included semi-palmated sandpipers and white-rumped sandpipers. Care is needed to tell these birds from dunlins or little stints, their common relatives. They all feed along muddy margins of lakes and seashore, and plumage characteristics and bill length are vital clues to their identity. You'll need a good bird book or knowledgeable companion to help you sort out the common from the 'wow, look at that'! Akeragh Lough is private and must be viewed from the road.

Tacumshin and Lady's Island Lakes

These two birdwatching 'hotspots' lie on the coast of Wexford just south of the R736 and not far from Rosslare Harbour. Tacumshin lies to the west of Lady's Island Lake and is open to the sea. Lady's Island Lake, on the other hand, is enclosed and is rather brackish in nature. Both are havens for wintering and migrant waders and wildfowl but also have a reputation for attracting rare birds, especially from North America.

Tacumshin has large areas of saltmarsh and mudflats, with some of the more characteristic plants of these habitats, including glasswort, sea-blite and eel-grass. This latter species is a favourite food of the brent geese that frequent Tacumshin in the winter. These geese, no bigger than a mallard duck, are unique among Britain's geese in having an all-black face. In world terms these are rare birds, about 20,000 of this, the pale-bellied race, spending the winter in Ireland. At this season, also look for ducks, while in autumn, a wide range of waders is the highlight. Lady's Island Lake is comparatively shallow and its waters have important populations of brackish-tolerant pondweeds.

Cottonweed – an attractive plant more usually associated with southern European shores – grows on the dry land, and terns nest here in the summer months. Autumn sees the arrival of migrant waders and September and October are the months to search for transatlantic visitors.

Wexford Wildfowl Reserve

This reserve lies on the north shore of Wexford harbour and is a site of major importance for wintering birds, especially wildfowl. Turn off the R742 to Gorey Road for the reserve. The area comprises a mixture of reclaimed pasture, with meadows prone to flooding, and saltmarsh. Waders and ducks are abundant but it is for the Greenland white-fronted geese that the area is best known. The reserve is open all year and there are walks and an observation tower.

The saltmarsh can be seen from the embankment wall, and good views can be had of many of the birds. The white-fronted geese fly over the wall at dawn and dusk. The observation tower gives views over the grazing pastures favoured by the geese.

Connemara National Park

Situated near Letterfrack, this national park has a nature trail and visitor centre providing detailed information about the blanket bog, woodland and heathland habitats found within the boundaries. Letterfrack is on the N59 in coastal Galway, 40 miles (64km) northwest of Galway.

The blanket bog has all the characteristic plant species: bog myrtle, cottongrass, bog asphodel, sundew and cross-leaved heath in the wetter areas, with heather and heath in drier spots. Snipe and

PEACE AND QUIET

meadow pipits breed in these areas and several species of birds of prey hunt here from time to time.

The Burren

This small area, near the west coast of Clare, is a mecca for botanists. Indeed, few of the more seriously inclined fail to make a pilgrimage at least once in their lifetimes.

The landscape of the Burren is comparatively young by geological standards: glaciation last affected the area as recently as 15,000 years ago. Much of the rock has been eroded flat, and slightly acidic rainwater has etched and worn gullies into its surface. Thus the famous limestone 'pavements' were formed and a wealth of plants now grow in the crevices and hollows.

The reason for the Burren's importance as a botanical site is the curious juxtaposition of species normally found in Arctic or Alpine settings growing almost at sea level alongside plants usually associated with the Mediterranean, southern Europe and the Azores.

The time to visit the Burren is in May and June, when the flowers put on a superb display of colour. Spring gentian, bloody cranesbill, hoary rock-rose, early purple orchid, eyebrights and mountain avens are widespread, while specialities include dark-red helleborine and dense-flowered orchid, the latter more characteristically a

Mediterranean species. A careful search of the gullies and crevices will reveal a wealth of ferns. Wetter areas, including turloughs, may harbour the delicately flowered fen violet.

The Burren is in Co Clare, northwest of Limerick. Corkscrew Hill, on the Lisdoonvarna to Ballyvaughan road, gives excellent views over the area. For particularly good examples of limestone pavements, try visiting Poulsallagh near Lisdoonvarna or Black Head, west of Ballyvaughan, where you should find all the typical flowers. Woodlands are somewhat unusual in the Burren, but at Poulavallan and Mullagh More there are some examples; the latter site also has turlough habitat.

Cliffs of Moher

Lying on the Clare coast west of Ennistymon, the Cliffs of Moher have some of the most dramatic and sheer cliffs in Europe; they are also among the highest. Although the views alone make a visit worthwhile, during the summer months the cliffs are home to vast numbers of seabirds: puffins, guillemots, razorbills, kittiwakes and fulmars all throng the ledges and overhangs and provide excellent views for those with binoculars and a head for heights.

Guillemots breed in large colonies, hundreds of birds often lined up on a ledge side-by-side. Kittiwakes also prefer this precarious niche, while razorbills favour boulders and crevices in the rocks in which to nest. Puffins, on the other hand, nest in burrows which they excavate with their powerful bills.

Pontoon

Nestling between Loughs Conn and Cullin, Pontoon, in Co Mayo, offers an interesting range of habitats to the visiting naturalist. To reach Pontoon, turn west of the main Ballina–Castlebar road at Foxford. Apart from the lake margins and birds of the open water, there is woodland (comparatively scarce in the west of Ireland) with a range of birds. The road which separates the two loughs allows good views over the water. Park at the eastern end to see the Pontoon Woods. Both Lough Cullin and Lough Conn provide good opportunities to see common scoters: the area is one of the most important breeding sites for these seaducks in Ireland.

The Burren's limestone pavement

In spring, the males are a distinctive and attractive sight with largely black plumage and yellowish-orange on the bill. The females are a rather drab, brown colour and are less conspicuous.

Pontoon Woods consist mostly of oak and holly, a woodland mixture characteristic of the western coast of Ireland, which is strongly influenced by the Atlantic. The ground flora is rich and woodland birds include sparrowhawks and treecreepers.

Downpatrick Head

Lying on the north coast of Mayo, Downpatrick Head offers superb cliff scenery combined with the opportunity to see breeding seabirds in the summer months, and migrants, especially in autumn. To reach it, drive north from Ballina to Ballycastle and then take minor roads to the headland. On the cliffs are fulmars, razorbills and guillemots, as

well as choughs, which nest in caves eroded into the sandstone. The passage of migrating seabirds in autumn can be even more dramatic than the breeding species. Birds are driven closest to land during northwesterly gales at Downpatrick, and in September and October, under ideal conditions, shearwaters, kittiwakes, Leach's petrels, gannets and seaducks stream by.

Glenveagh National Park
Situated near Letterkenny in Co Donegal, Glenveagh comprises woodland, lake, bog and moorland, with an interpretive centre and nature trail to help visitors get the most from the national park. The comparatively pollution-free air means that lichens and mosses thrive in the woodland,

and a rich understorey of plants has developed. Among the birds, redstarts and wood warblers are summer visitors to the area and the trilling song of the latter species is a delight in spring. You are quite likely to see red deer in open areas of the park.

Peatlands Country Park
The park is sited near the southwest shore of Lough Neagh and has excellent areas of bog and woodland. All the characteristic species of these habitats are present, together with some rare and unusual ones. To reach it, take exit 13 on the M1 and head east. In boggy areas, look for *Sphagnum* mosses, cottongrass, bog myrtle,

Downpatrick Head stands against all the force of the Atlantic

bilberry, sundews and
bladderworts, as well as bog
rosemary, a local and
declining species. Dragonflies
breed in the pools and waders
and wildfowl are occasionally
present.

The woodlands have a good
range of birds, including
treecreepers, jays and
sparrowhawks. Several
species of butterflies can be
found in the clearings.

Lough Neagh and Oxford Island

Lough Neagh is a shallow
freshwater lake, 15 miles
(25km) long and over 9 miles
(14km) wide: the largest lake in
the British Isles. The reed-
fringed margins and open
water are the haunt of wildfowl
and waders, and wintering
populations numbering tens of
thousands have been counted
for species such as tufted duck
and pochard.

Even during the summer,
Lough Neagh is by no means
quiet: great crested grebes,
tufted ducks, common terns
and black-headed gulls are
always present, many nesting
in the area. In early spring,
pairs of grebes can be seen
displaying to each other on the
open water. However, in the
autumn, numbers of ducks
begin to build up and by the
winter, whooper and Bewick's
swans have arrived.

One of the best places to view
Lough Neagh is Oxford Island,
near Lurgan, just off the M1 at
junction 10. Not only can the
waters and reedbeds be
viewed from a path and a
birdwatching hide, but there

are also hay meadows to add
to the habitat variety. These
harbour corncrakes in spring
and summer.

Downpatrick

Quoile Pondage near
Downpatrick has excellent
areas of open water, marsh
and woodland with breeding
birds such as snipe and
redshank and winter visitors
such as geese.

Near Downpatrick, there are
good opportunities for
watching birds at sea at St
John's Point and Ballyquintin
Point. At the former location in
particular, gannets,
shearwaters and sometimes
even skuas stream by during
onshore gales and both sites
are resting spots for migrant
landbirds.

Strangford Lough

Lying between Downpatrick
and Belfast, this huge sea
lough has, at low tide, vast
areas of mudflats exposed.
These are an ideal feeding
ground for waders and
wildfowl, and large numbers of
birds of many species can be
seen. In winter, pale-bellied
brent geese pass time on the
lough, which also has a very
large common seal population
and breeding grey seals. The
lough can be viewed from
numerous spots, including
Castle Espie and The Dorn,
near Portaferry.

Rathlin Island

This island lies off the north
coast of Antrim and can be
reached by boat from
Ballycastle. As with all trips
like this, the journey can be

every bit as exciting as the things you might see. Although the breeding seabirds are a highlight of any visit during the summer months, there are also meadow flowers to look at and seals offshore.

Between Bull Point and the West Lighthouse, look for kittiwakes, puffins, guillemots and razorbills. Each species has its own nesting requirement: puffins nest in burrows in the grassy slopes, razorbills hide in caves and under boulders while guillemots and kittiwakes nest on bare ledges.

Giant's Causeway

A geologist's dream, the Giant's Causeway is an official World Heritage Site. This extraordinary natural phenomenon consists of thousands of basalt columns. Some of the columns are over 30 feet (10 metres) tall and comprise basalt intrusions formed during unusual cooling conditions of this igneous rock. In addition to its obvious geological and scenic interest, however, the Giant's Causeway is of interest to the naturalist.

Rocky shores in the vicinity are feeding sites for rock pipits, redshanks, purple sandpipers and turnstones, while the cliffs are the haunt of choughs, which also occasionally feed on the seashore. Offshore, seabirds such as kittiwakes, gannets and auks can often be seen. The Causeway lies on the north coast, northeast of Coleraine.

Antrim

Within easy reach of Antrim are several interesting sites. Randalstown Forest, to the west of the town, is a mixture of plantation woodland and natural, wet woodland. Deer can be seen and the shores of the lough attract wildfowl and waders. Interesting woodland can also be found at Rea's Wood and Shane's Castle, both of which are on the shores of the lough on the edge of Antrim. Look for interesting woodland flowers and birds and wintering wildfowl around the lough margins.

Glenariff

Visitors to the Glens of Antrim can find beautiful scenery and interesting wildlife in the vicinity of Glenariff. The Glenariff Lakes – a series of small, upland loughs – and the adjacent Forest Park, harbour bog flowers, wildfowl and woodland birds, while Glenariff Forest Waterfalls are spectacularly beautiful in their own right. The humid air of the latter site encourages a rich variety of mosses and liverworts which thrive in the damp atmosphere.

Lough Foyle

Situated west of Limavady, in Co Londonderry, the shores and mudflats of Lough Foyle are a major site for migrant and wintering waders and wildfowl. The area can be viewed from many points, but Magilligan Point (where interesting sand dune formations can be found) and Eglinton are especially good.

FOOD AND DRINK

Quantity rather than quality has tended to be the key characteristic of Irish food, but matters are improving. The finest restaurants make inspired use of superb home produce, notably seafood including salmon, sea trout, oysters and mussels, good beef and lamb, and game.

Meals

The most reliably good meal in the Republic is an 'Irish breakfast' and its Northern Ireland equivalent, the 'Ulster fry'. This usually consists of fruit juice and/or cereal or porridge, followed by a plate of all or any of the following: bacon, chipolatas, black or white pudding (a sort of sausage), egg, tomato, mushrooms. This usually comes with wheaten or soda bread – delicious, often homemade wholemeal bread – and toast; occasionally with potato cake, rather like a soft, thick pancake.

Celebrating the Atlantic's oysters

Pubs are happy to serve tea and coffee, and many do at least simple food such as sandwiches. Tourist menus, offering lower-priced meals usually early in the evening, are increasingly common; and you can often get a filling and relatively cheap 'high tea', combining a simple cooked dish such as fish and chips with bread, jam and tea.

Shopping for Food

One of Ireland's best-kept secrets is its range of farmhouse cheeses. These are stocked by some groceries, delicatessens and supermarkets, and you can sometimes buy direct from the maker. They make a good lunch with fresh bread – bakery is one culinary art that has not been forgotten.

Reservations

Many good restaurants are in out-of-the-way places, and may open only if there is a demand; so phone first to make a reservation. Most close for a day each week, often Sunday, and for part of the year.

FOOD AND DRINK/SHOPPING/ACCOMMODATION

Drink

The pub is the undisputed hub of social life. Few Irish pubs have any pretensions, but what might seem a joyless drinking den is transformed by the friendly atmosphere.

Most Irish drink whiskey and beer brewed in Ireland itself (it's whiskey not whisky in Ireland). The best-known Irish drink is Guinness, a smooth, near-black, bittersweet beer with a creamy off-white head, made in Dublin since 1759. Then there's whiskey; some 15 brands, including the fine matured malts produced by Jameson's, Gilbey's and the world's oldest (legal) whiskey distillery, Bushmills.

SHOPPING

Tourist centres have gift shops selling everything from Irish linen to Connemara marble ashtrays to handmade Irish lace or Aran sweaters. In many parts of Ireland, visitors are encouraged to watch craftspeople at work. There is no obligation or pressure to buy, but be warned, the process is seductive.

Waterford Crystal is the best known of several Irish crystal manufacturers which offer factory tours; sometimes you can pick up cheaper seconds in the factory shops. In Belleek, Co Fermanagh, you can watch fine porcelain being handpainted. There are several places to watch weaving, including tweed in Donegal and Ardara, both in Co Donegal, and wool and mohair in Avoca, Co Wicklow, and Graignamanagh, Co Kilkenny.

The town of Kilkenny is the home of the attractive Kilkenny Design Centre, which also has a shop in Dublin; and several craftspeople welcome visitors (the tourist office can supply details).

Reclaiming Sales Tax

If you buy something in Ireland to take home with you, and you leave within two months of making the purchase, you may be able to claim a refund of the sales tax (VAT). This does not apply to British visitors to Northern Ireland. If you are a non-EC visitor, you can reclaim the VAT regardless of the cost of the item, as long as the shop operates a refund scheme. You will need a passport or other form of identification to show in the shop.

If you are from another EC country, you can get back the VAT on more expensive items, if the shop operates a refund scheme.

ACCOMMODATION

This guide gives regional selections of accommodation divided into price ranges. The price bands for Dublin are:

Expensive – IR£80 plus; Medium – IR£35 plus; Cheap – IR£20–IR£30. For other parts of Ireland, the price bands are: Expensive – IR£/£45 plus; Medium – IR£/£20 plus; Cheap – below IR£/£20. These prices are approximate.

Some establishments offer lower rates out of season, or special package deals. Expect to pay a supplement for single occupancy.

Types of Accommodation

Hotels Some hotels in this guide have star ratings: these are places which, on application, have been inspected and approved by the AA. The stars indicate the range of facilities.

Guesthouses (GH) Some are scarcely distinguishable from small hotels, but have more limited facilities.

Farmhouses (FH) A family home on a working farm, offering bed and breakfast accommodation.

Town and country homes (T&C) Private, often period houses with limited guest accommodation, run in country house style – breakfasts and dinners eaten at a communal table, for example.

Self-catering is another option. There are a number of purpose-built 'villages' in popular tourist areas, and some country estates have cottages to let; you can even rent a whole manor house, with staff. For details, contact the national tourist boards.

Reservations

If you are planning to stay in Dublin, it is sensible to reserve your accommodation. Elsewhere, the smaller good hotels and upmarket bed-and-breakfast places get booked up in high season. Many establishments close for part of the year, some for six months or more.

ENTERTAINMENT

There is a strong sense in Ireland that life should be as enjoyable as possible and that its pleasures are to be shared. Outside the cities, the main source of entertainment is the pub, a place for anecdotes and perhaps some singing. Many towns have a local theatre group, or attract touring productions; and nearly every community holds at least one festival a year.

Irish Music

Irish music is a vigorous, living tradition. Musicians play a variety of instruments – not so much that symbol of Ireland, the harp, but the fiddle, flute, tin whistle, accordion and guitar as well as two distinctively Irish instruments, the *uillean* pipes – like bagpipes, but inflated by bellows rather than the player's puff – and *bodhran* (pronounced 'boe-rawn' – a goatskin drum).

Apart from sessions in the pubs – look out for a *fleadh* (pronounced 'flah'), a festival organised by one of the 200 branches of Comhaltas Ceoltóirí Eireann (say 'coaltas keoltori ayran'); or you may be asked to a *ceilidh*, a party with music and dancing.

WEATHER AND WHEN TO GO

First, the bad news: it rains a lot – all through the year, sometimes for days on end, and particularly in the west. On the other hand, the rain is often what the Irish call 'soft', and the overall climate is gentle, even benign, without harsh extremes of heat and cold. July and August are the warmest months, with average temperatures around 14–16 degrees Centigrade (57–61 degrees Fahrenheit) though sometimes rising to around 24 degrees Centigrade (75 degrees Fahrenheit); the coldest are January and February, at around 7 degrees Centigrade (45 degrees Fahrenheit). However, spring (April/May) is often drier than summer; and September and October may be wetter (but are beautiful months as the trees turn colour and the hedgerows glow with wild fuchsia and hawthorn berries). Both are good times to see some of the major sites, which get very crowded in July and August.

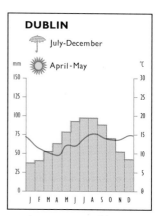

HOW TO BE A LOCAL

The Irish are used to tourists and their strange ways. Good humour and a tradition of hospitality, not to mention an astute appreciation of the economic advantages of tourism, combine to make them welcoming and tolerant. You will not be made to feel uncomfortable or excluded because you are an outsider, as long as you behave with good manners, good humour and generosity – valued characteristics in this highly sociable society.

One of the clichés about the Irish is their easy-going, even indolent nature, and it's true that time is less of a tyrant in Ireland. If you are used to hustle and bustle and to getting things done quickly, you may need to curb your impatience. After all, unless you are travelling on business, people will assume you are there to wind down and enjoy yourself. That most Irish of arts, conversation, is likely to prove one of the most memorable aspects of your visit. Being a good listener is important, both to gauge the attitudes of the speaker – particularly in Northern Ireland, or when sex or religion is the topic – and because talking is often a succession of performances. Storytelling lives on in the guise of anecdotes, some of them developed specially for the tourist. There is a tendency to tell visitors what they want to

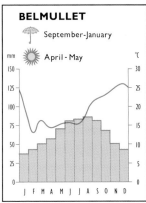

BELMULLET

September-January

April - May

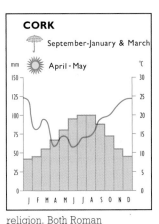

CORK

September-January & March

April - May

hear (or what the teller thinks they do), perhaps tongue-in-cheek to see if they will believe it; but the motive is not malicious, just a bit of devilment, a gentle teasing. Humour tends to the ironic, and jokes are woven into the conversation rather than produced like rabbits out of a hat.

If you are a good raconteur, you should find an appreciative audience as long as you avoid offensive humour (including jokes about the Irish, and anything smutty), don't boast (for example, about the number of fish you have caught that day) and don't mimic or insult Ireland or the Irish. Avoid pontificating about the Troubles in Northern Ireland, particularly when in the North; unless you know your companions well, it is best to limit any comment, if the subject arises, to one of regret for the situation. Northern Ireland apart, the two topics about which you must be sensitive are sex and

religion. Both Roman Catholicism and the various forms of Protestantism in Ireland condemn liberal attitudes towards sex, and issues such as abortion and divorce arouse strong feelings. Whatever their private behaviour, in public most Irish support the churches' attitudes. Religion in Ireland is complex, a matter of allegiances as much as beliefs. In Northern Ireland, great significance is read into someone's religion (though not that of visitors). Various means are used to establish what it is – the school they attended, their home address, even their names – without asking outright, which would be breaking a fundamental taboo. For fascinating insights into this and many other aspects of Northern Irish society, read Dervla Murphy's book on her travels in Northern Ireland in the 1970s, *A Place Apart*. In the South, politics is a fairly safe subject; few people have strongly felt loyalties to a particular party, and personalities rather than policies dominate. Political discussion often revolves around politicians' behaviour, provoking amusement or mild exasperation. If you want to pick up on the latest issue and learn a few key names, read the Irish press or watch the television news. It's also worth watching Gay Byrne's television programme, *The Late Late Show* – hugely popular and also influential in airing previously taboo issues. Finally, it will be helpful if you are acquainted with the basics of Irish history and culture, especially its literature, if only because one of the perennial topics of conversation among the Irish is – the Irish. They are highly conscious of their own national background and identity, and will respond to visitors who are able to share their interest.

CHILDREN

Ireland is a land of young people – nearly one in three of the Republic's population is under 15 years old. With a few exceptions, hotels and other types of accommodation welcome children, though it is always worth checking first. The main beach resorts are geared to family holidays, and have amusement parks and leisure centres. There are a few residential summer camps in the Republic, for 8–17-year-olds, offering various sports facilities with qualified teaching staff (Bord Fáilte can supply details).

TIGHT BUDGET

When To Go
● Avoid high season (July to mid-September), when air and ferry fares to Ireland and accommodation prices are at their highest.

Where To Go
● Spend at least part of your stay in Northern Ireland – it's generally cheaper.
● If you want to spend several days in Dublin, consider staying in a hostel (several have two-bedded rooms and there is no age limit – but ask the tourist office for a list of approved hostels), or in a B&B in one of the seaside towns on the DART line.
● University cities usually have a greater range of lower-priced eating places catering to the student market, and more budget accommodation.

Getting Around
● Consider renting a car in the North, where tariffs are cheaper – but make sure the insurance covers you for the Republic, if you intend crossing the border.
● Bring your own car over on a ferry – you can get special package deals including the sea crossing and vouchers for B&B.
● Combine public rail or bus transport for long-distance travel with cycling or hitch-hiking to overcome the lack of local public transport (An Oige, the Irish Youth Hostel Association, offers package deals for cycling, rail and hostel holidays).
● Combine transport and

accommodation – rent a horsedrawn caravan, or a cruiser.

● Take guided bus tours – for example, from Dublin, and from Killarney round the Ring of Kerry.

Where To Stay

● Opt for B&B accommodation in farmhouses or guesthouses, or stay in hostels, or rent a cottage or apartment. There are plenty of good campsites.

● Travel with a friend – most types of accommodation have twin-bedded rooms, and make a charge for single occupancy.

Eating Out

● Eat a hearty Irish breakfast and have a high tea – cheaper than dinner.

● If you like an aperitif, buy your own duty-free liquor on the trip over: all alcohol is expensive in the Republic.

Derby Day, the Curragh – a major occasion

SPECIAL EVENTS

Both the national tourist boards publish annual listings. The following is a selection:

March

St Patrick's Day, 17 March: celebrations throughout Ireland.

Easter

Irish Grand National at Fairyhouse, Easter Monday.

April

World Irish Dancing Championships, Cork. International Folk Dance Festival of Ireland, Cobh.

May

Cork International Choral and Folk Dance Festival. Pan Celtic International Festival, Killarney.

June

GPA Music in Great Irish Houses Festival. Bloomsday, Dublin, 16 June: in honour of James Joyce. Irish Derby, at The Curragh.

July

Orangemen's Day 12 July –
parades in Belfast.
Ulster Harp Derby – flat race
at Down Royal Racecourse.
Kerrygold Dublin Horse Show.

August

O' Carolan Folk, Harp and
Traditional Irish Music
Festival, Keadue.
Puck Fair, Killorglin.
Connemara Pony Show,
Clifden.
Fleadh Cheoil: the main annual
traditional music festival,
varying venue.

September

International Oyster Festival,
Galway.

October

Cork International Film
Festival.
Wexford Opera Festival.

November

Belfast Festival – one of the
UK's biggest arts festivals.

SPORT

Both spectator sports and
sporting activities of various
kinds are popular in Ireland.
For information contact the
national tourist boards. The
following are the main sports.
Irish games Hurling, in which
sides of 15 players play with
wooden sticks and a ball, and
Gaelic football, also 15 a side,
are potentially fast and furious.
Both are particularly common
in the southern counties of the
Republic. Road bowls, played
(illegally) along public roads in
West Cork and South Armagh,
are the occasion of much
betting.

Racing Horseracing is hugely
popular, and major meetings
are high points in the national
social calendar. Ireland is the
main European breeding
ground for thoroughbreds.
Steeplechasing was invented
in Co Cork in 1752, by two men
who decided to race their
horses across country between
two churches. Flat racing is an
even older tradition, centred
on The Curragh, in Co Kildare.
Classic races in the Republic
include the 2,000 and 1,000
Guineas, the Irish Derby, the
Oaks and the St Leger. Betting
can reach phenomenal levels.
Greyhound racing is also
popular.
Fishing Ireland has some of
the best and most varied
fishing in Europe. Both tourist
boards produce brochures.
Golf Ireland has several of the
finest golf courses in the world,
many in superb not to say
distracting natural settings. A
number of tour operators offer
golfing packages. Green fees
are generally reasonable, but
they vary: the southwest is
more pricey.
Sailing The two main centres
are the southwest coast, from
Youghal round to Dingle, and
Lough Derg, near Limerick.
Bord Fáilte produces a leaflet.
Walking There are several
long-distance footpaths including
the Ulster, Wicklow, Kerry and
Dingle Ways. Those in the
Republic are often
inadequately waymarked and a
map is essential; unfortunately,
although the Republic is
currently being remapped at a
1:50,000 scale, some areas are
not yet covered.

DIRECTORY

Arriving

By air The four international airports are Dublin, Shannon, Cork and, in the North, Belfast International (Aldergrove). The busiest is Dublin, but the majority of North American visitors fly into Shannon (16 miles/26km from Limerick). The state-owned carrier Aer Lingus runs scheduled services from 10 UK airports, and connecting inland flights from Dublin. Ryanair flies direct from the UK (but not from Heathrow or Gatwick) to nine airports. You can fly direct to Belfast International on scheduled flights from most UK airports and from Amsterdam and Paris; and from North America by charter flights. There are also direct flights to Belfast's City Airport from numerous British airports. Most airports have taxi ranks. A frequent express bus service runs between Dublin Airport and the Central Bus Station and major city hotels and also from Cork Airport into the city, Shannon Airport to Limerick, and Belfast International into Belfast.

Aer Lingus offices

Australia: Level 5, 36 Carrington Street, NSW 2000 (tel: (02) 299 6211); **Republic of Ireland**: 42 Grafton St, Dublin 2 (tel: (01) 377777); **UK**: Aer Lingus House, 83 Staines Road, Hounslow, Middlesex (tel: (081) 569 5555) or 223 Regent St, London W1; **US**: 122 East 42nd Street, New York 10168 (tel: (212) 557/1090).

By sea Ferry services run all year between several Irish ports and both Britain and Northern France.

By bus National Express and Irish Bus run an integrated coach service, Supabus, between a number of towns in Britain and the Republic. Some routes are seasonal. Slattery's runs a coach service integrated with B&I Line ferries linking southern England with southern and western Ireland. Dodds Coaches and Ulsterbus run a service from London to Belfast

DIRECTORY

via the Stranraer–Larne ferry.
By rail British Rail's InterCity
Ireland services are integrated
with Irish Rail in the Republic.
Entry formalities No passport
needed if you are a British
citizen born in the UK and
travelling from Britain. Other
EC visitors must have a
passport or suitable identity
documents. All other
nationalities need a passport,
and a very few need visas.
Pets Ireland is part of the
British Isles quarantine area.
Pets resident in Britain for at
least six months can be taken
to Ireland without any need for
quarantine. Animals from other
places must go into quarantine.

Bicycles

Bringing your own Most
airlines allow a bicycle as part
of a passenger's baggage;
check if there are special
requirements. Ferries may
make a small charge. You may
not be able to buy compatible

tubes and tyres in Ireland.
Renting The two main
suppliers in the Republic are
Raleigh Ireland, which has
'Rent-a-Bike' dealers in about
60 locations; and The Bike
Store, in Dublin, Cork,
Limerick and Rosslare, which
allows bicycles to be rented at
one outlet and returned to
another. In Northern Ireland,
nearly 20 shops rent out
bicycles. Information sheets
are available from both
national tourist boards.

Caravanning, Camping and Cruising

You can get lists of caravan
and camping parks from both
national tourist boards; those in
Bord Fáilte's brochure have
been inspected and graded.
You don't have to stay on
official sites; farmers may be
willing to let you camp in their
fields. There are package

Tune in to the Irish Harp

deals including car ferry and caravan hire. Horsedrawn caravans can be hired through CIE Tours International. You can rent cruisers and sometimes narrow boats on the Shannon, the Grand Canal and the River Barrow and, in Northern Ireland, Lough Erne; the season runs from mid-March to the end of October. Both national tourist boards supply lists of approved boat rental companies.

Chemist see Pharmacies

Crime
Theft, including stealing cars or property from cars, is the main crime to beware. Mugging is largely unknown outside some districts of Dublin, but large gatherings anywhere will attract petty thieves. Generally, though, visitors to Ireland, and particularly to Northern Ireland, are extremely unlikely to be the victims of crime.

Customs Regulations
Standard EC customs regulations apply when travelling between the Republic or Northern Ireland and another EC country, and if crossing the border between the two. Travellers may import or export goods for their personal use, up to certain limits depending on whether the goods were bought in ordinary shops (tax paid) or duty-free shops.

Disabled People
In the Republic and Northern Ireland, disabled drivers can park free of charge if the vehicle displays an Orange Badge. For details of accommodation accessible to people with mobility problems, contact the national tourist boards.

In the Republic
The Irish Tourist Board (Bord Fáilte) provides an accommodation guide especially for disabled persons published in conjunction with The National Rehabilitation Board, 24–25 Clyde Road, Ballsbridge, Dublin 2. This organisation have also published an access guide to Dublin and offer advice and help for disabled visitors. Wheelchair hire is available from the Irish Wheelchair Association, Blackheath Drive, Clontarf, Dublin 3.
Cars with hand controls can be rented from Hertz, 19 Hogan Place, Dublin 2 or Avis, 1 Hanover Street, Dublin 2.

In Northern Ireland
Useful addresses for disabled visitors to Northern Ireland include the Northern Ireland Council on Disability, 2 Annadale Avenue, Belfast BT7 3JR and the British Red Cross Society, 1st Floor, University Street, Belfast BT7 1HP.

Driving
AA offices The main AA offices are at Rockhill, Blackrock, Dublin (tel: (01) 2833555); 12 Emmet Place, Cork (tel: (021) 276922); and Fanum House, 108–110 Great Victoria Street, Belfast (tel: (0232) 328924).
Breakdown If the car is rented, contact the rental company. If

DIRECTORY

it's your own car, and you are a member of the Automobile Association or one of the AIT (Alliance International de Tourisme) driving clubs, you can call on the AA rescue service (run by the Automobile Association of Ireland in the Republic). The RAC operates a similar service for its members but only in Northern Ireland.

Car rental Renting a car in the Republic is expensive compared to Northern Ireland, though rates vary; smaller local firms often offer cheaper deals than the large international companies but may not let you pick the car up in one place and return it in another. The national tourist boards can supply lists of companies. The cheapest method is to book a fly-drive or rail-ferry-drive inclusive package.

Crossing the border There are 19 approved crossing points. Many other roads have been made impassable to deter smuggling and more sinister cross-border activities; if you are caught trying to cross by an unapproved road, you could face penalties. There are few formalities at frontier posts for private motorists, but take your vehicle registration book with you.

Documents required You will need a valid driving licence (with an English-language translation if you wish to rent a car) plus, if bringing a vehicle in, its registration book, with a letter of authorisation from the owner if he or she isn't accompanying the vehicle; see also **Insurance**. Your car, and

any trailer, should carry a nationality sticker. In the Republic, you may not allow an Irish resident to drive your vehicle, other than a garage hand with your written permission.

Driving in Ireland Drive on the left. The Republic has three road classifications: National Primary (prefix N, number 1–25), National Secondary (prefix N, number over 50) and Regional (prefix R). These are no reliable indicators of the width or surface quality – some primary roads are little better than country lanes. There are no motorways apart from short stretches north and west of Dublin. Reckon on an average speed of 30mph (48kph) when calculating journey times by car. Potential hazards in the Republic are loose chippings, livestock, and the relaxed attitude of Dublin drivers to red traffic lights. Northern Ireland also has three road classifications: motorways, A-roads and B-roads. The major roads are fast and well maintained, and seldom congested though checkpoints are a potential cause of delay.

Fuel Fuel stations in villages in the Republic usually stay open till around 20.00 hrs, and open after Mass on Sundays. In the North, 24-hour stations are fairly common, and many stay open on Sundays. Fuel is cheaper in Northern Ireland than the Republic.

Insurance Full comprehensive cover is advisable. If you intend crossing the border, check that your insurance

Youghal's spectacular beach is matched only by its sunsets

covers you in both the Republic and Northern Ireland.

Parking Dublin, Cork, Galway and several other towns and cities operate a parking disc system instead of or in addition to coin meters. Discs carrying instructions for use are available from local retail outlets and fuel stations. In Northern Ireland, many town centres have control zones, indicated by yellow signs warning that cars must not be left unattended.

Road signs Notoriously inadequate in the Republic – road signs are often absent, or broken off, or twisted, so expect to get lost and have to ask for directions. When signs do exist, they are usually in both English and Irish, except in some staunchly Irish-speaking areas. Distances are expressed in miles on the older road signs – black on white – and in kilometres on the new, green signs. In Northern Ireland, distances on the road signs are given in miles.

Seatbelts must be worn by drivers (except when reversing) and front-seat passengers.

Speed limits In the Republic, the limits are 30mph (48kph) in built-up areas and 55mph (88kph) elsewhere unless otherwise indicated; for non-articulated vehicles with one trailer, the maximum is 40mph (64kph). In Northern Ireland, the limits are 30mph (48kph) in built-up areas, 60mph (96kph) in country areas, and 70mph (113kph) on dual carriageways and motorways, unless otherwise indicated; for trailers, the maximum is usually 40mph (64kph).

DIRECTORY

Electricity

220 volts AC (50 cycles) is standard. Sockets for small appliances are the three-pin flat or two-pin round wall types.

Embassies and Consulates

Embassies in the Republic of Ireland:

Australia Fitzwilton House, Wilton Terrace, Dublin 2 (tel: (01) 761517)

Canada 65 St Stephen's Green, Dublin 2 (tel: (01) 781988)

UK 31 Merrion Road, Dublin 4 (tel: (01) 695211)

US 42 Elgin Road, Dublin 4 (tel: (01) 688777)

Consular offices for Northern Ireland:

Australia High Commission Australia House, The Strand, London WC2B 4LA (tel: (071) 379 4334)

Canada High Commission Macdonald House, 1 Grosvenor Square, London W1X 0AB (tel: (071) 629 9492).

Ornate iron door grill, Dublin

New Zealand High Commission New Zealand House, Haymarket, London SW1Y 4TQ (tel (071) 930 8422) **US** Queens House, 14 Queen Street, Belfast 1 (tel: (0232) 328239)

Emergency Telephone Numbers

In both the Republic and Northern Ireland, dial 999 for police, fire or ambulance.

Entertainment Information

Tourist offices (see below) carry current information about entertainments in their area. Both national tourist boards produce brochures listing the year's events. Newspapers such as the *Irish Times* and the *Cork Examiner* carry listings and advertisements.

Entry Formalities see Arriving

Genealogical Research

If you have Irish ancestry and want to trace your roots, you can undertake the research yourself or employ a professional genealogist. Both national tourist boards can supply details of reputable research companies and useful sources.

Health Regulations

There are no special health requirements or regulations for visitors to the Republic or Northern Ireland. It's best to take out medical insurance though EC visitors are covered by a reciprocal agreement. If you want to rely on this, you must bring Form E111 with you – contact your social security office for details. UK nationals do not need this form.

Holidays (Public and Religious)

(R) Republic only;
(NI) Northern Ireland only
New Year's Day: 1 January;
St Patrick's Day: 17 March;
Good Friday; Easter Monday; May Day: first Monday in May;
Spring Bank Holiday (NI): last Monday in May; **June Holiday** (R): first Monday in June;
Orangemen's Day (NI): 12 July;
August Holiday (R): first Monday in August; **Late Summer Holiday** (NI): last Monday in August; **October Holiday** (R): last Monday in October; **Christmas Day**: 25 December; **St Stephen's Day (Boxing Day)**: 26 December

Lost Property

Report serious losses – passport, credit cards, etc – to the police. For lost passports, inform your embassy which will be able to issue emergency documents. Embassies may be able to help with emergency funds if travellers' cheques are lost or stolen. Restaurants and other public places are often helpful and honest in keeping lost articles.

Media

In the Republic, there are four national morning newspapers – the excellent *Irish Times*, the middle-market *Irish Independent*, the *Irish Press* and the *Cork Examiner* – as well as three evening papers; the Sunday papers include the *Sunday Tribune*, useful for arts and restaurant and hotel reviews. Provincial newspapers are a great way of getting a feel for the area. Until recently, all broadcasting was run by the state-owned Radio Telefís Eireann (RTE), but there are now several independent local radio stations. The two homegrown television channels are still RTE-run. British television and radio broadcasts are received in many areas.

In Northern Ireland, the main daily newspaper is the evening *Belfast Telegraph*; the morning papers are the Unionist *News Letter* and Republican *Irish News*. As in the Republic, television viewers have a choice of six channels. There are five British national radio channels, the local BBC station Radio Ulster and some independent, mainly pop music stations (useful for traffic and weather reports).

Money Matters

The monetary units are (in the Republic) the Irish pound (punt), abbreviated as IR£, and (in Northern Ireland) the pound sterling (£), each divided into 100 pence. These are not interchangeable.

Banks are the best place to change money. Normal opening hours are 10.00–12.30, 13.30–15.00hrs (15.30hrs in Northern Ireland), weekdays only. Most banks in Dublin stay open till 17.00hrs on Thursdays. Foreign exchange counters in the main airports give decent rates: Belfast, open daily, 07.00–20.00hrs (22.00hrs on Saturday and Sunday); Dublin, open 06.45–22.00hrs in summer, 07.30–22.30hrs in winter; Shannon, to service all flights;

and Cork, open on weekdays all year and at weekends in summer.

Credit cards In the Republic, cards carrying the Eurocard symbol and American Express and Diners Club are generally accepted, though not by some restaurants and smaller independent retailers and fuel stations. In Northern Ireland, cards other than the Eurocard type are of limited use outside the main towns. Personal cheques can be cashed using a Eurocheque card. When staying in B&B establishments, expect to pay by cash.

Opening Times

Museums and tourist sites
Times vary, and are subject to change. Always check with a local tourist office before making a special journey. Many places close from October to March or have very limited opening; but most major sights are open all year.

Pubs In the Republic: Monday to Saturday, 10.30–23.30hrs in summer, 10.30–23.00hrs in winter, and Sunday, 12.30–14.00hrs and 16.00–23.00hrs. In Northern Ireland: Monday to Saturday, 11.30–23.00hrs; on Sundays, 12.30–14.30hrs and 19.00–22.00hrs.

Shopping Standard times are 09.00–17.30 or 18.00hrs, Monday to Saturday. Small towns (and all towns in Northern Ireland, except Belfast) have an early closing day. Late-night shopping, to 20.00 or 21.00hrs on Thursday and/or Friday evenings, is common.

Personal Safety

Parts of Dublin are risky (see the introduction to that city), and some suburban areas of Belfast, southern Co Armagh and the area round Coalisland, Co Tyrone, are more likely to see sectarian violence; but, generally speaking, the whole of Ireland is exceptionally safe. Hitch-hiking is common in the Republic. Natural dangers are also relatively few, though swimmers should beware of sea currents.

Pharmacies

These usually stock a wide range of goods including cosmetics and camera film. When closed, most display on their doors the address of the nearest open pharmacy, but you may not find one open on a Sunday. In an emergency, contact the nearest hospital. Contraceptives may not be easy to find in more remote parts of the Republic.

Places of Worship

Ireland is a land of churches, both Catholic and Protestant, and of holy places, some of them internationally famous. The Marian shrine at Knock, Co Mayo, attracts over a million visitors a year. Some 93 per cent of the Republic's population is Roman Catholic, and there are few non-Christian places of worship.

Police

In the Republic: Garda Síochána (say 'sheekawnah') in black-and-blue uniforms, most unarmed. In Northern Ireland: Royal Ulster Constabulary (RUC), in green uniforms.

Post Office

In the Republic, standard post office opening times are 09.00–17.30hrs, Monday to Saturday, but sub-post offices close at 13.00hrs one day a week. The General Post Office in O'Connell Street, Dublin, is open Monday to Saturday, 08.00–20.00hrs, and 10.30–18.00hrs on Sundays and bank holidays. Post boxes are green; Republic of Ireland stamps must be used.

In Northern Ireland, standard opening times are 09.00–18.00hrs, Monday to Friday, and 09.00–12.30hrs on Saturdays. Post boxes are red, and British stamps must be used.

Public Transport

In the Republic, local public transport is limited: many locals hitch-hike.

In Northern Ireland, although local public transport is better than in the Republic, you will still be restricted without a car. An Emerald Card gives unlimited bus and rail travel throughout the whole of Ireland, for eight-day or 15-day periods. For information on guided tours in the Republic contact CIE Tours International, at 35 Lower Abbey Street, Dublin (tel: (01) 731100); for Northern Ireland contact Belfast's Ulsterbus Travel Centre, Glengall Street (tel: (0232) 320011).

Air Aer Lingus and Ryanair run flights from Dublin to other airports in Ireland. Aer Arann runs several daily flights between the Aran Islands and Galway.

Interior, Olympia Theatre, Dublin

Bus In the Republic, Bus Eireann operates a network of express bus routes serving most of the country, though some run only in summer. In the greater Dublin area, bus services are controlled by Dublin Bus: unpredictable but sometimes useful. A four-day Dublin Explorer ticket also covers travel on Dublin's suburban rail network.

In Northern Ireland, the bus network is run by Ulsterbus, with express links between Belfast and 20 towns. Unlimited travel tickets, for one or seven days, are available.

Rail In the Republic, a limited network operates between major towns and cities. For information, contact a CIE office or Iarnród Eireann (tel: (01) 366222). The Dublin area has its own, very useful Rapid Transit system, DART.

DIRECTORY

Unlimited rail travel tickets are available to visitors: the seven-day Runabout for services within Northern Ireland and to Dundalk (valid in April to October); and the Irish Rover, for travel throughout Ireland for eight or 15 days.

Taxis Available in major cities, at taxi stands or outside hotels, and at main rail stations, ports and airports. Check that the cab has a meter, and negotiate fares in advance for long distances. In Belfast, some black cabs are shared by customers; some operate rather like buses, shuttling their passengers between the city centre and the outlying suburbs.

Jaunting cars means pony-drawn traps, which offer rides in some picturesque areas.

Senior Citizens

Many car rental companies give discounts to customers over 50 or 55, as do some hotels and a few tourist attractions. Some tour companies offer special spring and autumn package deals.

Student and Youth Travel

The Irish Youth Hostel Association (An Oige, 39 Mountjoy Square, Dublin 1 (tel: (01) 363111) has nearly 50 hostels dotted throughout the Republic, some in beautiful old buildings and glorious locations. Six hostels are run by the Youth Hostel Association of Northern Ireland (YHANI, 56 Bradbury Place, Belfast BT7 1RU tel: (0232) 324733). Another 76 hostels in the Republic belong to the Independent Hostel

Owners group (contact IHO Information Office, Dooey Hostel, Glencolumbkille, Co Donegal tel: (073) 30130). A small number, most in the west of Ireland and all approved by Bord Fáilte, belong to Irish Budget Hostels (contact them at Doolin Village, Co Clare tel: (065) 74006).

Members of An Oige or the Youth Hostel Federation can get fare reductions on some ferry crossings. Holders of a valid International Student Identity Card should contact their local student travel agency, or the USIT offices in Dublin or Limerick, or the tourist boards, to obtain a Travelsave Stamp, which entitles them to travel discounts. Both Eurail and Transalpino passes (for people up to 26 years old) can be used in Ireland.

Telephones

It is cheaper to phone direct rather than through the operator, and to use a private phone rather than a public pay phone, except in hotels when you are liable to be charged extra. For telephone numbers and other information, consult the telephone directories. The cheapest rates apply at weekends and from 18.00 to 08.00hrs on weekdays. Local calls in the Republic are charged at a standard rate regardless of duration; otherwise, telephoning in the Republic may seem expensive.

To call a number in Ireland, first dial the access code: Australia 0011; Canada 011;

New Zealand 00; UK (for the Republic) 010. Then dial 353 for the Republic or 44 for Northern Ireland, and then the full number (omitting the first zero).

If calling a Dublin number from the UK: for a 6-digit number dial 010 353 12. For a 7-digit number omit 2.

Note: Dublin numbers are in the process of changing from 6 to 7 digits: if in doubt, ring Directory Enquiries (see number below).

For international calls out of Ireland, except to Britain, dial 16 in the Republic or 010 in Northern Ireland, wait for a new tone, then dial the country code: Australia 61; Canada 1; New Zealand 64; US 1. Then dial the full number, omitting the first zero. To call the UK from the Republic, dial 03 and then the full number. In the Republic, dial 114 for the international operator; for directory enquiries, including Northern Ireland numbers, dial 190.

In Northern Ireland dial 100 for the operator, 192 for directory enquiries including numbers in the Republic, 153 for international directory enquiries, and 155 for the international operator.

Call boxes New-style glass and metal boxes are being introduced to replace the old ones, which are blue and cream in the Republic and red in Northern Ireland. Phones using cards (which can be bought at retail outlets such as newsagents) are also on the increase.

Dialling tones Two short tones repeated at regular intervals mean the phone is ringing; long tones interspersed with short pauses mean the line is busy; an uninterrupted tone means the line is faulty or defunct.

The harbour at Clifden

DIRECTORY

Time

Both the Republic and Northern Ireland follow Greenwich Mean Time, but with clocks put forward one hour from late March to late October, as in Britain. Time differences with other countries are: Australia add eight to 10 hours; Canada subtract three and a half to nine hours; New Zealand add 12 hours; US subtract five to 11 hours.

Tipping

Hotels and restaurants often include service on bills; otherwise, you can leave a tip of around 10–15 per cent. Hotel porters expect a tip of around 50 pence a bag; taxi drivers around 10 per cent of the fare.

Toilets

Public lavatories may be scruffy or worse, except those at tourist sites. Use one in a hotel, department store or pub.

Tourist Offices

Both the Irish Tourist Board (Bord Fáilte) and the Northern Ireland Tourist Board maintain offices abroad. These can supply a wide range of information to help you plan your visit, including large numbers of brochures and guides, most of them free. Irish Tourist Board (Bord Fáilte):

Australia 5th Level, 36 Carrington Street, Sydney, NSW 2000 (tel: (02) 299 6177).
Canada 160 Bloor Street, East Suite 934, Toronto, Ontario M4W 1B9 (tel: (416) 929 2777).
UK 150 New Bond Street, London W1Y 0AQ (tel: (071) 493 3201); 53 Castle Street, Belfast BT1 1GH (tel: (0232) 327888).
US 757 Third Avenue, New York, NY 10017 (tel: (212) 418 0800).
Northern Ireland Tourist Board:
Britain Northern Ireland Business Centre, 11 Berkeley Street, London W1X 5AD (tel: (071) 493 0601).
Republic of Ireland 16 Nassau Street, Dublin 2 (tel: (01) 6791977).
US Suite 500, 276 Fifth Avenue, New York, NY 1001 (tel: (212) 686 6250).

In the Republic itself, there are some 100 tourist information offices (look for a white letter *i* on a green background), nearly 30 of them open throughout the year. Standard times are from Monday to Friday all day, and Saturday mornings.

A tourist board leaflet gives full details. Tourist offices on both sides of the border offer an accommodation reservation service to visitors calling in person, for a small charge to cover telephone costs; you will also be asked for a 10 per cent deposit, which will be deducted from your accommodation bill. The Central Reservations Service, 14 Upper O'Connell Street, Dublin 1 (tel: (01) 841765) can handle advance bookings. The Northern Ireland Tourist Board's head office is in Belfast, at St Anne's Court, North Street, Belfast (tel: (0232) 231221). There are another 30 or so local tourist offices, most open all year; opening times vary. A tourist board leaflet gives full details.

LANGUAGE

The Republic has two official languages, English and Irish. Everyone speaks English, though you are likely to hear Irish in the Gaeltacht areas of the west and north, where you may find some road signs in Irish only.

This is how to say some of the words you may come across:

Bord Fáilte (literally board of welcomes – the Irish Tourist Board) 'bord fawlty'

ceilidh (traditional dance night) 'kaylee'

Gaeilge (the Irish language) 'gale-geh'

Gaeltacht (Irish speaking country) – 'gale-tackt'

Garda Síochána (police) 'gawrdah sheekawnah'

fleadh (traditional music evening) 'flah'

Taoiseach (Prime Minister) 'teeshock'

Numbers
1 a haon ('a hay-on')
2 a dó ('a doe')
3 a trí ('a tree')
4 a ceathair ('a ca-hir')
5 a cuíg ('a koo-ig')
6 a sé ('a shay')
7 a seacht ('a shocked')
8 a hocht ('a huct')
9 a naoi ('a neigh')
10 a deich ('a de')

Socialising
beer (Guinness type) pórtar ('porther')
cheers sláinte ('slawn-te')

good day lá maith ('law mah')
good bye slán ('slawn')
good night oíche mhaith ('ee-ha vah')
how are you? fine, thanks conas taoi? go maith, slán a bheas tú ('co-nus tee? goh mah, slawn a ves too')
please más é do thoil é ('maws eh duh hull eh')
pub tábhairne ('taw-er-nay')
thanks gura maith agat ('gurrah mah a-gut')
water uisce ('ishkek')
whiskey fuiscí ('fwishgee')
yes sea ('shah')

Long Room, Trinity College Library

INDEX

INDEX/ACKNOWLEDGEMENTS

The Automobile Association would like to thank the AA in Ireland, and the following photographers, libraries and associations for their assistance in the preparation of this book.

DEREK FORSS took all the photographs in this book (© AA Photo Library) except:

BORD FAILTE 31 Newgrange, 35 Jerpoint Abbey, 37 Kilkenny Castle, 48 Cathedral Limerick, 51 Bantry House, 52 Castletownshend, 62 Galway City.

DEREK FORSS 46 Rock of Cashel, 54 Three Sisters & Smerwick Harbour, 55 Lough Leane, 64 Cliffs of Moher, 69 Achill, 83 Giant's Causeway, 92 Mountains of Mourne, 101 The Burren, 123 Clifden.

MARY EVANS PICTURE LIBRARY 15 Parnell.

NATURE PHOTOGRAPHERS LTD 97 Corncrake (P R Sterry), 98 Valentia Island, 102 Downpatrick Head (R A Chapman).

NORTHERN IRELAND TOURIST BOARD 73 Belfast City Hall, 78 Transport Museum, 79 Belfast Botanic Gardens, 80 Belfast: Crown Liquor Saloon, 81 Fleadh Ceoil, 86 Ulster American Folk Park, 91 Hillsborough.

ZEFA PICTURE LIBRARY UK LTD Cover Connemara.

Author's Acknowledgements

Brigid Avison thanks the following people and organisations for their help: Anne Moore of the Northern Ireland Tourist Board, Ellen Redmond and Mark Rowlette of Bord Fáilte, also John and Carola Moran, the Morrisons and Bonita Stanley.